CONTEMPLATIVE BIBLE READING

Experiencing God Through Scripture

A SPIRITUAL FORMATION STUDY GUIDE
BY RICHARD PEACE

NAVPRESS
BRINGING TRUTH TO LIFE
NavPress Publishing Group
P.O. Box 35001, Colorado Springs, Colorado 80935

Visit the NavPress web site at: http://www.navpress.com/

ISBN: 1-57683-108-6

Cover illustration by: Wood River Media, Inc.

(Originally published in 1996, this edition of *Contemplative Bible Reading* has been fully revised and updated.)

Printed in the United States of America

1 2 3 4 5 6 7 8 9 10 / 02 01 00 99 98

Contents

SPIRITUAL FORMATION STUDY GUIDES
BY RICHARD PEACE

Spiritual Journaling:
Recording Your Journey Toward God

Spiritual Autobiography:
Discovering and Sharing Your Spiritual Story

Contemplative Bible Reading:
Experiencing God Through Scripture

Meditative Prayer:
Entering God's Presence

Acknowledgments

I have had the privilege of working with the Bible in a variety of ways throughout my life, from writing small group Bible study materials to teaching the Bible in both church and seminary settings. Even my doctoral work was in biblical studies. However, I discovered contemplative Bible reading (its more common name is the Latin *lectio divina*) rather recently.

Hence, I need to acknowledge my sources because I feel myself to be such a novice at *lectio*. Norvene Vest's book *Bible Reading for Spiritual Growth* provides the basic structure for doing group *lectio*. *Too Deep for Words* by Thelma Hall has been a helpful guide. Dom Jean Leclercq made monastic culture come wonderfully alive in *The Love of Learning*, and *The Desire for God* by Brian Taylor made Benedictine spirituality clear and contemporary. William Shannon's book *Seeking the Face of God* is the best resource for explaining the whole process.

I especially want to thank Father Bill Lowe of the Parish of the Messiah in Newton, Massachusetts, for pointing me in the right direction in exploring *lectio divina*. He came to me for consultation on small groups and I received, in return, consultation on *lectio divina*. I also want to thank my wife, Judy Boppell Peace, who is involved in all my writing projects, but in this series went one step further by working through the drafts in detail. Her ability to identify just the right word has made this book more precise and theologically clear. Finally, I want to thank Father John Kerdiejus, S. J., a spiritual friend and counselor who first introduced me to *lectio divina* and to so much more in the spiritual life.

How to Use This Guide

Introduction

I have always been fascinated by how the Bible works in us to bring about transformation. First, the Bible forms our minds. Its core concepts have the ring of truth and thus help define our worldview. Second, the Bible helps us express our emotions so we can develop into more whole people than we would be otherwise. Third, the Bible shapes our behavior by giving us abundant examples of outcomes—good, bad, and indifferent—so that we learn to distinguish between behavior that brings light and behavior that brings darkness. Finally (and perhaps most important of all), the Bible tells us that love is at the core of life. God is love. We are loved. We are to love. And so we are empowered to live life with gusto. How all this (and so much more) works together in us, over time, is the mystery. The testimony of countless men and women through the ages is that it does work.

What's it all about?

This guide will help you learn a spiritual discipline called contemplative Bible reading. Contemplative Bible reading is a way to approach Scripture not just to learn about God but to engage in conversation with him. You can use this guide to do contemplative Bible reading with a group or just on your own.

How will we know what to do?

The process of contemplative Bible reading is explained in the introduction (pages 11-20). Session one (pages 21-30) gives complete instructions for each aspect of the preparatory Bible study, and session two (pages 31-40) provides instructions for contemplative Bible reading in small group.

What will I learn?

You will learn a method of Bible study that the church has used for over 1,500 years and that unlocks Scripture in profound ways. You also will learn a style of prayer that flows directly from Scripture and opens up new ways of hearing God. Finally, you will gain a series of insights into the nature of the spiritual life drawn from the various passages of Scripture you will study.

Is this course intended only for church members?
No—anyone can join. God is active in every life whether we acknowledge that fact or not. This group will help those not yet actively following God to see and understand his activity in their lives, and thus to respond to him in new ways. This course is written in ordinary language so that anyone can participate. When theological terms are used, they usually are explained.

Can I do this without a group?
Certainly. Contemplative Bible reading was designed for individuals. This guide will teach you methods for both group and private *lectio divina.* You can use the individual method for each of the Bible passages in this guide. If you like, you can then go on to use this method for other passages of your choosing.

If I meet with a group, how long will the group last?
That depends upon the group. There is material in this book for ten group sessions: five Bible studies and five contemplative Bible reading exercises. However, you can combine both parts into one session and do the course in five weeks.

There is also material for five sessions in which you can practice contemplative Bible reading on your own between group meetings. These individual exercises are optional, but you will find them beneficial.

If I work on my own, how long will this study take?
You can proceed at whatever pace seems right for you. There are a total of fifteen exercises in the book. You can do one, two, or even more per week as your schedule permits.

How long does each session last?
If you meet with a group, ninety minutes per session is best. However, if necessary, you can complete a group session in sixty minutes. If you work on your own, you probably can complete a session in forty-five minutes if you are pressed for time.

What if I don't know much about Bible study?
No problem. The Bible study notes will give you the necessary background information.

Who leads the meetings?
Anyone can lead. The symbol Ⓛ in each session denotes instructions for the leader. Beginning on page 105, there are notes about small group leadership in general as well as specific leader's notes for each session.

As in anything else, the more experience the better. If you have an experienced small group leader, take advantage of his or her skills.

What kind of commitment is needed?
Each person needs to be open to the process of contemplative Bible reading and be willing to open themselves to the text.

What happens to the group when it finishes this book?
The group is invited to continue, using another book in the Spiritual Formation series. See page 4 for the other titles.

A Small Group Covenant
The best way to launch any small group is with clear and agreed-upon expectations. While you may wish to add others based on the special characteristics of your group, the following commitments are a good place to start.

- *Attendance*: I agree to be at the meeting each week unless a genuine emergency arises.

- *Preparation*: I will practice *lectio* during the week as I am able and share with the group some of what I find.

- *Participation*: I will enter enthusiastically into the group discussion and sharing. I will participate in the group *lectio* experiences willingly.

- *Prayer*: I will pray for the members of my small group and for our experience together.

- *Confidentiality*: I will not share with anyone outside of the group what is said during the group session.

- *Honesty*: I will be forthright and truthful in what I say.
- *Openness*: I will be candid with others in appropriate ways. I will allow others the freedom to be open in ways appropriate for them.
- *Respect*: I will not judge others, give advice, or criticize.
- *Care*: I will be open to the needs of each person in appropriate ways.

Signed: ____

An Introduction to Contemplative Bible Reading

The Bible stands at the center of all traditions of Christian spirituality. The question is not whether one should study the Bible (many agree that we should). The question is how to study the Bible so that it transforms us. This is where approaches vary. Contemplative Bible reading is one such approach that can help us access Scripture in a life-changing way.

Contemplative Bible reading is one of the oldest methods of Bible study. Its traditional name is *lectio divina*, a Latin phrase (pronounced lex-ee-oh di-vee-nuh) that can be translated "divine reading," "spiritual reading," or "sacred reading." The terms "contemplative Bible reading" and "*lectio divina*" (or *lectio*) will be used interchangeably in this book.

The History of Lectio Divina

Lectio divina has been used for over 1,500 years. It is gaining popularity as more and more people are finding it a powerful way to nurture their spiritual lives. In the past (especially in the Protestant church), we have concentrated on the study of the Bible. As a result we have come to know a lot about the Bible. But we have not been very good at applying the Bible, much less hearing God through the Bible. *Lectio divina* is an approach that builds on serious Bible study but moves to new depths as we open ourselves to God through the Bible.

The early monks approached the Bible by means of *lectio divina*. It worked for them like this: During the time set aside for personal reading, prayer, and reflection, a monk would go to a private place and begin to repeat aloud a passage from Scripture. Often this was taken from the Psalms or Gospels. The monk spoke the passage out loud until he was struck by a particular word or phrase. Then he would stop and ponder this word or phrase, understanding it to be a word from God for him. This meditation (which is what he was doing) led naturally into prayer as the monk offered back to God what he heard. As he moved deeper and deeper into prayer he would come to the place where he rested in the presence of God. Such a state of contemplation was actively sought.

One of the first leaders to commend *lectio divina* as a spiritual exercise was Benedict, an Italian monk who lived in the fifth and sixth centuries (about 480-550). He wrote his *Rule for Monks* in A.D. 525, outlining what life in a monastery should be like. His *Rule* quickly became the standard text guiding the functioning of monasteries.

Benedict is sometimes credited with inventing the workday. In *Rule* he gives a detailed schedule (called an *horarium*) for a monastic day. In this schedule, *lectio divina* is so important that several hours each day are given over to it, and it was to be undertaken at the time of day when the monks had the most mental energy. When Benedict spoke of *lectio*, what he had in mind was that step in the process that involved "chewing" on the text. A monk would speak aloud the text and ruminate on the words he was hearing.

In the twelfth century, Guigo II, a French Carthusian monk, spoke of *lectio* as a process and not just a step. It was he who made it into the four-step exercise used in this book.

As we move out of an Enlightenment way of thinking, with its emphasis on the mind, into the Postmodern era, with its emphasis on the whole person, there is a growing desire to know the Bible in more than just a cognitive way. The fact that contemplative Bible reading has holiness of life as its objective is of great interest in our culture. Understanding the text is part of contemplative Bible reading, but the primary focus is on helping us to hear God's Word through the text. In fact, contemplative Bible reading is really a form of prayer, as will become clear through a description of the process.

The Process of Contemplative Bible Reading

Contemplative Bible reading is both a simple and a profound way to approach Scripture. It consists of a four-part movement, beginning with the text and ending in prayer. This style of Bible reading can be used by both individuals and groups.

The four steps that make up contemplative Bible reading are

- ❖ *Reading/Listening*: Read aloud a short passage of Scripture. As you read, listen for the word or phrase that speaks to you. What is the Spirit drawing your attention to?

- *Meditating*: Repeat aloud the word or phrase to which you are drawn. Make connections between it and your life. What is God saying to you by means of this word or phrase?

- *Praying*: Now take these thoughts and offer them back to God in prayer, giving thanks, asking for guidance, asking for forgiveness, and resting in God's love. What is God leading you to pray?

- *Contemplating*: Move from the activity of prayer to the stillness of contemplation. Simply rest in God's presence. Stay open to God. Listen to God. Remain in peace and silence before God. How is God revealing himself to you?

Each of these four steps of contemplative Bible reading will be discussed in more detail in the essays at the end of each *lectio* session. However, you will learn more about each step by practicing it rather than defining it. This is the aim of the small group sessions: to learn, together with a group of like-minded people, how to do contemplative Bible reading. In addition, you are invited to practice this process on your own during the week between small group sessions. Texts are suggested and guidance is given in each *lectio* session for what is called daily *lectio*.

The Experience of Contemplative Bible Reading

Here is an example of what takes place in each of the four steps.

- *Reading/Listening*: The text is Matthew 11:28-30:

  > *Come to me, all you who are weary and burdened, and I will give you rest. Take my yoke upon you and learn from me, for I am gentle and humble in heart, and you will find rest for your souls. For my yoke is easy and my burden is light.*

  As you read these words aloud, you are struck by the phrase "you who are weary and burdened." Your heart responds to these words. You are, indeed, weary and burdened.

- *Meditating*: Now you speak these words aloud. You turn them over in your mind: "you who are weary and burdened." Why are you so weary? Because of all the work you have done and all the work that is yet to be completed before you can rest. As you let these thoughts take hold in your mind you realize that this is not only a description of your present moment but a description of your whole life. Life has always felt burdensome to you. You always have needed to "get things done" because by your accomplishments you gain praise from others. And this praise from others has made you feel valued. You let these thoughts go where they lead you, staying in God's presence and coming back again and again to the phrase "you who are weary and burdened."

- *Praying*: Now you start formulating your prayer to God. In fact, it formulates itself even as you meditate on this phrase. You thank God for this insight into your life, for this new understanding of why you always feel so weary, so burdened. You ask God for guidance so you can put your work into perspective: doing what needs to be done, doing what God calls you to do, and knowing when to say "enough." You ask for a new sense of God's love for you that will free you from your need to gain affirmation from others. You praise God for loving you.

- *Contemplating*: As you remember again the love of God, you rest in that love. "I love you, Lord." With those words you sit in silence before God. It is an alert silence, however. You have no agenda. You have no further words. You have already prayed. You simply sit before God. What happens in this moment of contemplation is completely up to God.

When your attention begins to wander, you go back to the text and start the process over again, listening for a new word or phrase. You read it again, listening for what else God might have for you. Or you end your prayer experience with a "thank you" or "praise God" and enter into the tasks of the day, taking with you this sense of God's presence, this experience of God's love and guidance. This "presence" sits in the background as you greet others or start work on the report you must finish that day. It sustains you in your tasks. It softens you with others. It takes the edge off the urgency that so often makes you feel burdened. You live in the world of sense and time, but with the impression of eternity in your heart.

Group Lectio Divina

It is possible to use the contemplative Bible reading process in groups as well as individually. The name for this is group *lectio divina* (or group *lectio*). This is a five-step exercise led by a small group leader, which consists of multiple readings of a short text, individual reflection on that text, brief sharing of this reflection with the small group, and prayer for one another.

The method of group *lectio* that you will use is based on *Bible Reading for Spiritual Growth* by Norvene Vest (HarperSanFrancisco, 1993). You are encouraged to read for yourself her full description of group *lectio*. Particularly illuminating is Vest's ongoing case study of a small group learning to do *lectio* together.

The process of group *lectio* is as follows:

1. Prepare by quieting yourself to listen to God's Word.

2. Listen to the Word of God.

    - ❖ As the passage is read twice, listen for the word or phrase that strikes you. During the silence, repeat that phrase softly (or silently) to yourself.

    - ❖ Then, when invited, say aloud to the group this word or phrase without comment or elaboration.

3. Ask, "How is my life touched by this word?"

- ❖ The passage is read again. This is followed by personal meditation on how this word or phrase connects to your life.

- ❖ When invited, state in one or two sentences the connection between the phrase and your life.

4. Ask, "Is there an invitation for me to respond to?"

- ❖ After the passage is read a third time, ponder whether you are being encouraged to do something in response.

- ❖ Share this response briefly with the others.

5. Pray for one another to be able to respond.

- ❖ Pray briefly for the person on your right.

Further instructions for this process are given in session two (pages 31-40).

Group *lectio* differs somewhat from individual or daily *lectio* mainly because contemplation (step four) is not something one can order or organize. Contemplation simply happens—in various ways and at various times for various people. So group *lectio* ends with prayer for one another and not in a silent resting in the presence of God.

There is another difference between daily *lectio* and group *lectio*: the invitation to action. In individual *lectio*, during meditation you may or may not sense that God is calling you to respond in some deliberate way in the next day or two. But this is the essence of step three in group *lectio*. There is great power in asking God what is required of us. There is great power in sharing what we hear with others also, who then help us respond to this invitation by praying for us.

Despite these differences, group *lectio* contains the essence of contemplative Bible reading: hearing a short passage, listening for a word or phrase, meditating on this word or phrase, and opening yourself to God to respond as you are led. The added advantage of group *lectio* is that what you hear can be discussed immediately with others who also are listening for God. Furthermore, by speaking aloud the invitation you feel God is giving you, you make public your intentions and the group holds you accountable in a gentle way.

The premise of Spiritual Formation Study Guides is that, given our busy lifestyles, we are more apt to learn such disciplines in a group than on our own. This holds true for contemplative Bible reading. The experience of group *lectio* introduces us to the process. The practice of daily *lectio* deepens our understanding of the process. And the context of the small group both motivates us to practice *lectio* and gives us a forum in which to share what we hear from God.

Group *lectio* raises several issues. For one thing, does God always have something for us to do? Step three seems to assume so. It is important, therefore, to understand that while we may hear a call to action we also may hear a call to rest in God. Or our invitation might be to experience God's creation or to experience the love of God.

Second, how comfortable are you in discussing what is, fundamentally, an intimate relationship with God? It is one thing to open yourself to God; it is another to share it with others. Therefore, it is important to notice the way in which sharing is structured. In group *lectio*, what you are asked to share is minimal. When you read the complete instructions for group *lectio* in session two (pages 31-40), you will find that you are asked to say aloud only a few words or sentences. Furthermore, you always are given the option of "passing," that is, of saying nothing. Therefore, while public sharing lies at the heart of group *lectio*, it is not forced or excessive. However, as you grow in love and trust in your small group, you will find the power of mutual sharing. The group will receive your words as a gift; you will experience others' words as a gift. There will be mutual growth and encouragement. This is how we are meant to live the Christian life.

Bible Study and Lectio

One common reaction to *lectio divina* is that it seems to take away the objective study of Scripture and replace it with a highly subjective method of interpretation. Such a method has the potential to cause us to stray far from the original meaning of the text. This is a legitimate criticism and one that needs to be taken seriously. There has been an unfortunate history of making the Bible mean whatever a person wants it to mean. When one considers the range of behavior and ideas that Scripture is supposed to support—many of which contradict each other—the need for careful Bible study is clear. When examining Scripture the first question must always be, What did the passage mean to those who originally read it? The sole question can never be, What does the passage mean to me?

But subjectivism is not the only problem. The objective also can get out of hand. Too much Bible study these days has been reduced to a mere academic exercise in which hypotheses are weighed and tested, various interpretations are discussed, and in the end people know a lot more about a passage, but it makes little difference in how they live.

The choice ought not to be between dry scholasticism and irresponsible subjectivism. We need both approaches to Scripture. We need analysis and application. We need knowledge and insight. We need to listen with our minds and with our hearts. If the Bible is, as we claim, the inspired Word of God, then we need to approach it so as to understand what God is saying to us, and to hear God say this to us in the context of our lives.

Consequently, this book combines the benefits of both analytical and contemplative reading. Each passage is looked at twice. The first session on each passage is serious Bible study in which you will try to understand what the text is saying. This session contains background notes on the passage to help you read it in context. The second session then builds on this insight and (by means of *lectio*), inviting you to listen with your heart to what your head knows. Neither process is done to the exclusion of the other. This study attempts to give you a balanced experience of the Bible that takes seriously the need to analyze and the need to listen, the need to understand and the need to pray.

How the Sessions Work

Each of the ten sessions in this study guide contains a selection of the following modules:

- *Overview*: This section gives you a preview of what you will find in the session.

- *Open*: Your main aim in this exercise is to build relationships among group members. A group of acquaintances becomes a group of friends as you tell your stories to one another. Both the Bible study session and the *lectio* session contain "Open" exercises. If you are using this guide on your own, you may omit the "Open" exercises.

- *The Passage*: The Bible passage is printed out for you.

- *Analysis, Resonance, Prayer, Bible Study Notes*: The Bible study session includes these four sections. You will first examine the passage to see what it says, then consider how it resonates with your own experience, and finally pray. The notes offer background on the passage; you may read some or all of them during your discussion of "Analysis."

- *Group Lectio*: The *lectio* session contains a portion of the passage you analyzed in the previous session. The small group leader will guide you step by step through group *lectio* on this portion. If you are using this guide on your own, you can adapt the instructions simply by reading the passage aloud for yourself and omitting those instructions that are relevant only for groups.

- *Discussion*: The purpose of this final portion of the *lectio* session is to discuss both the experience of *lectio* and the outcomes. When you are first learning this method, you will want to focus on the process itself. Later, you may want to use this time for more discussion of personal outcomes. The time for the discussion section is adjustable. How long the group *lectio* takes will depend upon how many people you have in the group. Take as much time as you need for the group *lectio*, and use the remaining time for discussion. If you are using this guide on your own, you may omit this section.

- *Essay*: The essay at the end of each *lectio* session examines a different aspect of contemplative Bible reading. Each essay expands on some aspect of the process described in this introduction. The essays are to be read on your own, although some groups may choose to discuss them together.

- *Daily Lectio*: You will learn how to engage in contemplative Bible reading by practicing this discipline on your own. Suggestions will be given for texts that you can examine during the week between small group sessions.

SESSION ONE

Longing for God

A BIBLE STUDY ON PSALM 63

Group Note:
Leader's Notes for this session can be found on page 106.

Overview

If you are meeting with a group, you will introduce yourself in this session by talking about your experience of Bible study and your interest in the topic of contemplative Bible reading. You also will study Psalm 63, which speaks of our longing for God. In session two you will look at Psalm 63 again, this time focusing on verse one for your experience with *lectio divina*. The essay at the end of session two will provide an introduction to the role of centering prayer as you prepare to engage in contemplative Bible reading.

OPEN 20-30 MINUTES

Studying the Bible

Each of us brings to this group our own experience of the Bible. By way of introducing yourself to the group, think about the many ways you have encountered the Bible.

1. a. Introduce yourself to the group by briefly telling one amazing incident in your life or exciting experience you have had. (For example, you hiked through the Grand Tetons; or you were born in South Africa; or you reared four children; or you touched a shark while diving.)

   b. Give one reason why you came to this group.

2. In what ways have you learned about the Bible? Which has been the most meaningful for you?

   ❑ through sermons
   ❑ in Christian education classes
   ❑ through personal study
   ❑ through continuing education
   ❑ in small groups
   ❑ at a retreat
   ❑ in quiet times
   ❑ in a college or seminary class
   ❑ by reading commentaries
   ❑ through devotional reading
   ❑ in family readings
   ❑ as great literature
   ❑ other:

3. If possible, share one experience in which the Bible came alive for you in a special way.

THE PASSAGE 5 MINUTES

A psalm of David, when he was in the Desert of Judah.

1 O God, you are my God,
earnestly I seek you;
my soul thirsts for you,
my body longs for you,
in a dry and weary land
where there is no water.

2 I have seen you in the sanctuary
and beheld your power and your glory.
3 Because your love is better than life,
my lips will glorify you.
4 I will praise you as long as I live,
and in your name I will lift up my hands.
5 My soul will be satisfied as with the richest of foods;
with singing lips my mouth will praise you.

6 On my bed I remember you;
I think of you through the watches of the night.
7 Because you are my help,
I sing in the shadow of your wings.
8 My soul clings to you;
your right hand upholds me.

9 They who seek my life will be destroyed;
they will go down to the depths of the earth.
10 They will be given over to the sword
and become food for jackals.

11 But the king will rejoice in God;
all who swear by God's name will praise him,
while the mouths of liars will be silenced. (Psalm 63)

ANALYSIS 10-15 MINUTES

4. Using a word or a phrase, identify the theme of each of the four sections of this psalm:

   Verse 1

   Verses 2-5

   Verses 6-8

   Verses 9-11

Section One (Verse 1)

5. a. What is the central image David uses to describe his longing for God?

   b. Think about your worst experience of thirst. What does that teach you about the kind of longing David had for God?

   c. How does David describe his relationship with God?

Section Two (Verses 2-5)

6. a. What experiences does David name in which he has encountered God?

b. What are his various responses to God?

c. What is the outcome of this experience with God?

Section Three (Verses 6-8)

7. a. Why would night be a time of particular terror for David?

b. What does he do during the night?

c. What attitudes toward God enable him to get through the night? What images does he use to describe these attitudes?

Section Four (Verses 9-11)

8. a. Who do you suppose sought David's life?

b. What outcome does David visualize? What will be the fate of his enemies?

c. What will be the response of the friends of God?

RESONANCE 20-30 MINUTES

Longing for God

9. a. In what ways have you experienced a longing for God? Explain.

❑ a hunger to know God
❑ a thirst for spiritual things
❑ an uneasiness that is not satisfied by external things
❑ an intimation of God that whets your appetite
❑ an inner desire for the transcendent
❑ a holy restlessness
❑ a calling to be about God's work
❑ an urgency to grasp what is real
❑ a dream from God
❑ a pain that is too deep
❑ a longing to touch the life of God
❑ other:

b. How is God revealed in your life these days?

Experiencing God

10. a. In what ways have you experienced God?

❑ in Scripture
❑ in nature
❑ in prayer
❑ in worship
❑ in a dream
❑ in my meditation
❑ in inconsolable longing
❑ in relationships
❑ in contemplation
❑ in community with others
❑ through the still, small voice
❑ in deeds done for others
❑ in the events of life
❑ in a mystical experience
❑ in a sense of "oughtness"
❑ in the fruit of the Spirit
❑ other:

b. What ways of responding to God have been most meaningful?

- ❑ worship
- ❑ praise
- ❑ through words
- ❑ in fellowship
- ❑ in creative responses
- ❑ acting on others' behalf
- ❑ in turning from darkness
- ❑ singing
- ❑ in prayer
- ❑ in bodily action
- ❑ in quiet meditation
- ❑ in sharing God's story
- ❑ through spiritual disciplines
- ❑ in journaling
- ❑ in beholding the works and wonders of God
- ❑ other:

Night Terrors

11. a. What are nights like for you?

b. What problem does night present to you? How do you cope?

c. In what ways might David's words help you at night?

Life Destroyers

12. a. What are the names of those forces or powers that take life from you? (Examples include lust, addiction, lies, despair, hatred.)

b. How does David's vision of the End help us in resisting these life-taking forces?

PRAYER 5-10 MINUTES

13. Go around the group and ask each person to identify in thirty seconds or less one thing God has been saying to him or her personally through this study.

14. Go around the circle a second time and let each person pray for the small group member on his or her right, based on what that person just shared about the impact of the text. (If you are uncomfortable praying aloud, simply say, "I pass.")

BIBLE STUDY NOTES

Overview: David was in big trouble when he wrote this psalm. His son Absalom had mounted a coup to take over the throne, and David had fled into the desert (2 Samuel 15). In the midst of his distress, David's faith in and longing for God are apparent. Psalm 63 begins with longing (verse one) but ends with rejoicing (verse 11).

Psalm 63 focuses on several themes: longing for God, experience of God, terrors that confront us, forces that have the potential to undo us, and hope that sustains us in the midst of trial. Which of these connects most deeply with your life?

Verse 1: David's longing for God is so intense that he compares it to the kind of physical deprivation one feels in a desert without water. "A dry and weary land" is an apt description of the wild, hostile range of hills and deserts in the region between Jerusalem and the Jordan River. This physical language expresses how it really feels to desire God in the depth of one's being: it is a deep thirst. In what ways have you experienced longing for God?

Verse 2: David's flight into the desert has denied him access to the communal worship of God that took place at the temple. But he remembers what it was like. The "power" of God is the influence or force that God exerts. The "glory" is God's presence. Its substantial nature makes God so much more real than anything or anyone else. God's "weight" or "thickness" is a substance against which everything else is fleeting and inconsequential. Have you experienced worship to this degree? Who is God to you in worship?

Verses 3-4: What David remembers most of all is the special quality of God's "steadfast love" or "lovingkindness" (phrases used for the Hebrew word *chesedh*). This word is used frequently in the Hebrew Bible and is difficult to translate fully into English. It speaks of an enduring love on God's part, love that will not let you down, love that flows out of God's faithfulness in keeping promises made to us. This is a love so powerful that to know it is better than life itself. This is our goal in contemplation: to rest in the presence of that love. When we know we are loved by God, we are empowered by the joy that expresses itself in deep praise. How have you experienced God's love?

Verse 5: So satisfying is his experience of God in worship that David uses another physical image to express what it means to him. His soul is satisfied with the power, glory, and steadfast love of God as his body is satisfied when he eats the richest of foods. David's praise to God is expressed with his lips (through words), by his raised hands, and in his singing. How do you worship God?

Verses 6-8: Night in the desert is a dangerous time. It is not only a time when David is at risk from nocturnal creatures, but also a time when his enemies can sneak up on him. He does not sleep well; he must keep watch. But he is sustained during these lonely hours by his meditation, his remembrance of God. Two images express his confidence. God is to him like a bird sheltering its chick under its large, comforting wings. David is held in God's mighty hand where no harm can befall him.

Likewise, "night thoughts" may afflict us as we try to sleep; the anxieties we keep in check during the day emerge as troubling thoughts when we let down our guard. We remember tasks we have to complete, encounters that grieve us, fears that overwhelm us. David gives us a way to cope with night thoughts. We center our thoughts on God and not on these troubles. We give our anxiety over to God. We remember God. What night thoughts trouble you, and how might David's words help you?

Verses 9-11: His thoughts are on those enemies who stalk him by night. David envisions a future when all this is over: God vindicates him and destroys his enemies. His words anticipate the Christian hope that one day this world with all its woes will end. Jesus will return a second time and the world will be transformed into a new heaven and a new earth where righteousness prevails. David envisions a great battle, at the conclusion of which his dead enemies lie unburied on the battlefield where they are food for scavengers.

God's future is a great comfort. Though times may be hard now, we know that ultimately we have a home with God, and this makes it possible to go on. This is not "pie in the sky by and by," but a strong faith in God. What "enemies" (including lies, despair, addiction) plague you? How can David's words help you overcome those life-destroying forces?

Session Two

Longing for God

A *Lectio* Exercise on Psalm 63:1

Group Note:
Leader's Notes for this session can be found on page 108.

Overview

In the first session you studied Psalm 63, which speaks of our longing for God. Now you're going to look at Psalm 63 again, this time focusing on verse one for your experience with *lectio divina.* The essay at the end of this session addresses the role of centering prayer as you prepare to engage in contemplative Bible reading.

OPEN 20-30 MINUTES

Listening to God

Almost everyone prays. How, when, and why we pray varies greatly. What have your prayer experiences been like?

1. When you were a child, how did you pray? Are your memories of such prayer positive, negative, or neutral?

❑ at meals	❑ in Sunday school
❑ at church	❑ on my own
❑ with friends	❑ I heard others pray
❑ I didn't pray	❑ other:
❑ before going to sleep	

2. What is the most remarkable answer to prayer you have heard about or experienced?

3. What role does prayer play in your life now, if any?

GROUP *LECTIO* — 30-40 MINUTES

You will need three people to read the passage aloud. The leader will read the passage aloud twice, then later two different people will read. Agree on who will read the passage, then read over the instructions below so that you will know what to expect. If you don't understand something, ask for clarification.

Find a comfortable place to sit, preferably a straight-backed chair that will support you comfortably. Or sit on the floor with your spine straight if that is a familiar position for you.

1. Prepare. (Remember, Ⓛ represents instructions for the leader.)

Ⓛ Read the following words aloud, slowly:

> Sit in silence with your eyes closed. Straighten your spine, but let your body relax. Let your weight rest on the chair or the floor where you are sitting. Relax the muscles in your legs. Relax your arms. Relax your chest. Exhale deeply, and relax. Relax your throat. Relax your face. Inhale slowly, and listen to the breath as it enters your body. Listen to your breath as you breathe out.
>
> Focus on God. If you wish, you may pray a simple prayer as you breathe in and out, such as "Lord Jesus Christ, have mercy" or "Come, Lord Jesus." We ask the Holy Spirit to speak the Word of God to us, to show us what we need to see and hear through the Scripture. As we open ourselves to the spiritual world, we ask to be surrounded and protected by God's presence. We offer to God all the concerns we have brought with us today; we lay them in God's hands so we may hear God's Word clearly.

2. Listen.

Ⓛ Say, "Listen to the Word of God. Listen for a word or phrase that touches you." Then read the passage aloud, slowly:

> O God, you are my God,
> earnestly I seek you;

my soul thirsts for you,
    my body longs for you,
in a dry and weary land
    where there is no water. (Psalm 63:1)

Ⓛ After a brief pause, read the passage aloud again, slowly. Ask the group to repeat to themselves (silently) the word or phrase that touched them. Allow one minute of silence.

After the silence, say, "Let us share our words or phrases." Then begin by sharing aloud your own phrase.

Group: When it is your turn in the circle, speak your phrase aloud. Say only this word or phrase with no comments or elaboration. You may say, "I pass," if you wish, at any point in this process.

3. Ask.

Ⓛ Ask, "How is my life touched by this word?"

The second reader will now read the passage aloud, slowly.

Group: Consider how your word or phrase connects to your life. Sometimes this will be an idea or a thought; at other times it will be an image or some other impression. You will have two to three minutes of silence for this meditation.

Ⓛ After two or three minutes, say, "Let us share our reflections." Then begin by sharing your own thoughts on how the phrase you chose connects to your life.

Group: When it is your turn, share in one or two sentences the connection between your phrase and your life. Again, do not elaborate, explain, or justify what you sensed. One or two sentences are enough at this point.

4. Ask.

Ⓛ Ask, "Am I being invited to respond?"

The third reader will now read the passage aloud.

Group: Consider whether you are being invited to respond in some way in the next few days: "Am I being encouraged to do something?" You will have two to three minutes of silence for meditation.

Ⓛ After two or three minutes, say, "Let us share our invitation." Then begin by sharing, in one or two sentences, the invitation you sense from the passage.

Group: When it is your turn, share in one or two sentences, without elaboration, the invitation you have received from the passage. Listen carefully to what the person on your right says because you will pray for that person based upon what he or she has shared.

5. Pray.

Ⓛ Say, "Let us pray for one another to be enabled to respond to this invitation." Then pray for the person on your right.

Group: When your turn comes, pray briefly for the person on your right. You may pray aloud or silently. If you pray silently, say, "Amen," when you finish so the next person will begin praying.

DISCUSSION **10-20 MINUTES**

This may have been your first experience of group *lectio*. Think about the process itself.

Process

1. a. Was this a comfortable experience for you? Why, or why not?
   b. Was your word or phrase obvious? Not so obvious?
   c. Was finding connections easy or hard?
   d. Was the invitation to action easy or hard to discern?
   e. What was it like for you to pray? To be prayed for?
   f. What part of the process is unclear to you?

Experience

2. What happened for you in this exercise?

ESSAY

Centering: Preparation for Lectio

Before you begin a *lectio* exercise, it's usually necessary to take a few moments to focus your attention on God. Your aim is to let go of the issues and agendas that occupy your thoughts and move your mind to God. This is not always easy to do. Most of us live in an action-filled universe surrounded by distractions galore. When we come into our group, we bring with us all this internal baggage. Centering is a way to let go of our old agendas and give ourselves to a new agenda: openness to God.

There are two aspects of centering: the physical and the spiritual. How we position our bodies is important so that there is no physical impediment to prayer. How we position our minds is important so that we are focused on God and not on some other distracting issues.

The Physical

❖ *Seating*: It doesn't matter whether you sit or kneel or stand. The important thing is for your spine to be straight but not tense. "This posture is important, for it brings the body to attention. If we slump, the mind and spirit slump as well, and then we are not attentive to the Word."[1] If you are sitting, let your weight rest on the seat of a straight-backed chair with both your feet flat on the ground. Let the chair take your weight. The aim is to remain alert and attentive.

- *Muscles*: Relax tense muscles. You can be deliberate about this. Let the muscles in your legs relax. Feel your stomach muscles relax. Then relax your arms and chest. It is most important to relax the muscles in your throat. Tension collects there for a lot of people. Relax your face muscles. To know what muscle relaxation feels like, try tensing a muscle group and then releasing it. Then try letting it relax even beyond its natural resting point.

- *Breathing*: Slow your breathing. At this point you may use a centering prayer (see page 38), praying the first phrase as you breathe in and the second phrase as you breathe out.

The Spiritual

- *Pray*: Ask the Holy Spirit to guide your exercise, to lead you to those words you need to hear, to make connections between the Word of God and your life, and to open you to God. Pray also that as you open yourself to the spiritual world, you will be protected from evil and surrounded by God's power and presence.

- *Focus on God*: You may use an image, such as meeting Jesus on the road and talking with him, or sitting beside a pool or near a mountain and breathing in the presence of God. Or you may open yourself to God without image, simply praying in faith with expectation. Offer to God your concerns so that your focus is on God and not on your fears and problems. Ask God to take these burdens. You will sometimes find that certain issues reappear during the *lectio* exercise as the text speaks in response to them.

- *Use a centering prayer*: These are brief phrases the church has used for centuries to help believers focus on God. Examples include "Lord Jesus Christ, Son of God, have mercy on me, a sinner" (the so-called Jesus prayer); "Come, Lord Jesus, come"; "God, have mercy on me, a sinner!" (Luke 18:13); and "O God, you are my God." Find the words that seem best for you to pray. You might want to pray this prayer in rhythm with your breathing: as you inhale, pray, "Lord Jesus Christ," and as you exhale, pray, "Have mercy." The purpose of centering prayer is not to empty your mind of all conscious thought, but simply to empty it of distractions while you focus on God. It is an aid to being filled with the awareness of God.

When you engage in daily *lectio* on your own, it may be helpful for you to find the right place. There is something about "sacred space." These are environments in which we find the quiet, the peace, and the focus that enables us to reach out to God through *lectio*. This sort of space differs for different people. It may be a garden, a loft, a particular chair, or a chapel to which we go when we pray. Environment helps us focus.

You also want to find a place free of interruptions. This is true whether you are doing group *lectio* or daily *lectio*. Consider the ways you might be interrupted, and then think about how to deal with them before they happen. Get a babysitter to look after the kids during the group time, make sure the answering machine is on, schedule your time when you know everyone is away, and so on.

It's important to remember the aim of all this preparation: full attention to God, focus on God, and expectation that you are in the real presence of the living God.

Daily Lectio

As with other spiritual disciplines, you will only learn *lectio divina* through practice. If possible, take time during the week to read and pray in this way. You will need to find between fifteen and thirty minutes in a quiet space. Then follow the outline described on pages 13-14 and in the following summary.

- *Prepare*: Relax physically and focus spiritually. Center your thoughts on God. Pray for guidance.

- *Read/Listen*: Read the passage aloud to yourself. Read slowly and with openness.

- *Meditate*: When a word or phrase strikes you, stop and repeat it to yourself. Don't try to figure out why it has your attention. Be open to connections between the phrase and your life. Mull these over.

- *Pray*: Offer these thoughts to God. Respond to God. Don't worry about whether your prayer is profound or long. It may be only a word or two.

- *Contemplate*: Sit in silence before God. Listen. Be open to images or impressions.

- *Repeat*: Go back to the text when your mind starts to wander. Start reading again. Repeat the whole process.

- *Conclude*: Offer a word of thanks or praise to God.

The first story for you to investigate is in Exodus 3:1-12, when Moses meets God at the burning bush.

Moses was in a difficult place when this incident occurred. He was living in a remote area, working as a shepherd, looking after the flock of his father-in-law, Jethro. This was a far cry from his former life in Egypt. There he had been a prince; now he was a hired hand. At the time of this incident, Moses had been shepherding his father-in-law's sheep and goats for almost forty years. On this day he was going about his normal routine when he had a sudden, dramatic encounter with God.

We too know failure and fall, mediocrity and boredom, exile and pain, life in the wilderness. We know that it is more often at the bottom than at the top that God comes alive for us, when everything changes and we receive new hope, new vision, and a new task.

Work through this passage using the *lectio divina* method of study and prayer.

Note

1. Brian C. Taylor, *Spirituality for Everyday Life* (Collegeville, Minn.: The Liturgical Press, 1989), p. 64.

Session Three

The Call of Jesus

A Bible Study on John 1:29-42

Group Note:
Leader's Notes for this session can be found on page 109.

Overview

This session focuses on Jesus' invitation in John 1 to follow him. In this passage we read about the first encounter between Jesus and three of his twelve disciples: Andrew, Simon, and (probably) Philip. The invitation to follow that Jesus gave them is the same invitation he offers us today. We hear this invitation not just once but many times. In fact, Jesus urges us to follow him throughout our lives. Each time we hear that call anew we recommit ourselves to him.

You will have the opportunity in session three to consider your own response to Jesus' invitation, as well as to the title John gives him: Lamb of God. In addition, you will discuss the group covenant, which will serve as the guide to how you relate to one another as a group.

OPEN 20-30 MINUTES

Group Covenant

Every group needs ground rules by which it functions. This is particularly important in a group in which you share with others out of the intimacy of your relationship with God. Today you will begin by discussing a group covenant. A covenant is simply a way of agreeing to abide by a set of principles that foster openness, honesty, and love. Read the suggested covenant (pages 9-10), then discuss it.

1. Are there any ground rules you think should be deleted?

2. Any items to be amended or added?

3. When you all agree, sign your covenant, pray together, and offer this covenant to God.

THE PASSAGE 5 MINUTES

One of the first tasks in the ministry of Jesus was to appoint twelve individuals who would join him in his ministry. Jesus had many disciples, but to these twelve he gave the name apostles (Mark 3:14). In this passage we read about the first encounter between Jesus and three of the Twelve: Andrew, Simon, and (probably) Philip. In the same way that Jesus invited them to follow him, he urges us to follow him throughout our lives. Each time we hear that call anew we recommit ourselves to him.

29The next day John saw Jesus coming toward him and said,
"Look, the Lamb of God, who takes away the sin of the world!
30This is the one I meant when I said, 'A man who comes after
me has surpassed me because he was before me.' 31I myself did
not know him, but the reason I came baptizing with water was
that he might be revealed to Israel."

[32]Then John gave this testimony: "I saw the Spirit come
down from heaven as a dove and remain on him. [33]I would not
have known him, except that the one who sent me to baptize
with water told me, 'The man on whom you see the Spirit come
down and remain is he who will baptize with the Holy Spirit.'
[34]I have seen and I testify that this is the Son of God."
[35]The next day John was there again with two of his disciples. [36]When he saw Jesus passing by, he said, "Look, the
Lamb of God!"
[37]When the two disciples heard him say this, they followed
Jesus. [38]Turning around, Jesus saw them following and asked,
"What do you want?"
They said, "Rabbi" (which means Teacher), "where are you
staying?"
[39]"Come," he replied, "and you will see."
So they went and saw where he was staying, and spent that
day with him. It was about the tenth hour.
[40]Andrew, Simon Peter's brother, was one of the two who
heard what John had said and who had followed Jesus. [41]The
first thing Andrew did was to find his brother Simon and tell
him, "We have found the Messiah" (that is, the Christ). [42]And
he brought him to Jesus. Jesus looked at him and said, "You are
Simon son of John. You will be called Cephas" (which, when
translated, is Peter). (John 1:29-42)

ANALYSIS — 10-15 MINUTES

John the Baptist Announces Jesus (John 1:29-34)

4. a. What do you remember about John the Baptist? Who was he? What did he say and do?

   b. What two titles does John give to Jesus (one at the beginning of his testimony, the other at the end)? What do these titles mean?

   c. What do you know about Jesus from the testimony of John?

Two Disciples Follow Jesus (John 1:35-39)

5. a. What attracts these two to Jesus?

   b. What do they do and how does Jesus respond?

   c. What is the significance of their actions?

Andrew Brings Simon to Jesus (John 1:40-42)

6. a. What does Andrew tell Simon and why?

   b. How does Jesus respond to Simon?

RESONANCE

20-30 MINUTES

Who Is Jesus to You?

7. a. What title best sums up who Jesus is to you? Explain.

- ❑ Lord
- ❑ Master
- ❑ Savior
- ❑ Teacher
- ❑ Prophet
- ❑ Son of God
- ❑ Son of man
- ❑ Son of David
- ❑ Messiah
- ❑ Lamb of God
- ❑ other:

b. What do the twin titles Lamb of God and Son of God mean to you personally?

Following Jesus

8. a. When, if ever, did you consciously start following Jesus?

b. Why did you follow Jesus? Why do you still follow Jesus?

c. In what new ways is Jesus calling you to follow him?

Bringing Others to Jesus

9. a. Whom have you brought or might you bring to Jesus?

b. What have you discovered about yourself as a result of coming to Jesus?

PRAYER **5-10 MINUTES**

10. Let each person identify in thirty seconds or less one thing God has been saying to him or her personally through this study.

11. Go around the circle a second time and let each person pray for the small group member on his or her right, based on what that person just shared about the impact of the text.

BIBLE STUDY NOTES

Context: The two central figures in this account are John the Baptist and Jesus. We are witnessing John pass the torch to Jesus. John the Baptist has created quite a stir in Israel. He is the first prophet in Israel in over 300 years. As a result, the country is alive with excitement and anticipation. The crowds flock to John, many of them making a long and arduous journey to the wilderness around the Jordan River where he is baptizing. Once there, they listen eagerly to his message. It is not a comfortable one. John calls the people to repentance. He baptizes them in the Jordan for the forgiveness of sins. It is unheard of for Jews to be baptized in this way. The Jews understood themselves to be God's chosen people. The rite of baptism is something Gentiles undergo when becoming Jews. But so great is the sense of need (Israel has been a captive nation for generations) that they submit to baptism in great numbers.

Then along comes Jesus. He too is baptized even though John hesitates (but Jesus insists). In his baptism, Jesus identifies with the sins of the people, sins for which he soon will die. With the launching of Jesus' ministry at his baptism, John's role begins to diminish. He is the forerunner. Now the one he came to announce is here. His disciples now start to become Jesus' disciples.

Who do you follow? John the Baptist was a worthy master. His ministry pointed to God. But there are many other gurus that lead us away from God. Sometimes we follow individuals living or dead. Sometimes we follow principles or axioms like

"Making a buck" or "Every man for himself" or "If no one gets hurt, it is okay." Sometimes we unconsciously follow dark powers, such as addiction, anger, and pride. We too must choose whom or what we will follow.

Verses 29-31: Here John reveals why he baptizes: to announce the coming of Jesus. John also identifies who Jesus is: the Lamb of God. In Israel's sacrificial system, lambs were offered at the altar as substitutes for those bringing them. In a symbolic way, the people's sins were washed away by the blood of these lambs, who died in their place. Jesus would die in the place of not just one person but all persons for all times. He would be the final, ultimate, complete sacrifice.

Jesus gives himself for others. This is the ultimate demonstration of love. If we follow Christ, by implication we too are to relate to others not as people to be used, but as people to be loved. What does it mean to you to follow the Lamb of God?

Verses 32-34: Now Jesus is revealed to be not only the Lamb of God, but also the Son of God. This is a powerful assertion. In his baptism, Jesus reveals who he actually is. His was not just baptism with water, but baptism with the Holy Spirit.

Jesus is our link to God. He is not just a martyr who gives himself for others, worthy though this is. He is God's own Son. To know Jesus is to know God. In these verses we encounter the Trinity: God the Father, God the Son, and God the Holy Spirit.

Verses 35-39: Two of John the Baptist's disciples take an interest in Jesus at John's urging. One of these two disciples is named Andrew (verse 40); the other's name is not given. Some feel the second disciple might be John, the author of this Gospel, who appears anonymously at other points as "the beloved disciple." But it is more likely that the unnamed disciple is Philip (see verse 43), who is with Andrew on two other occasions in this Gospel (6:5-9; 12:21-22). The response of the two disciples is to follow Jesus. In the Gospel of John, "following" connotes discipleship. Jesus confirms their discipleship by inviting them to "Come and see." They then spend time with Jesus as befits new disciples. He has become their teacher, or rabbi.

People become interested in Jesus in many ways. First the testimony of a respected leader, John the Baptist, launches two people into discipleship. Then the testimony of a brother brings Simon to Jesus. How did you get interested in Jesus? How can you help others to find Jesus?

Session Four

The Call of Jesus

A *Lectio* Exercise on John 1:35-39

Group Note:
Leader's Notes for this session can be found on page 109.

Overview

Session three dealt with Jesus' invitation in John 1 to follow him. In addition to studying the passage and discussing your group covenant (if you are using this guide with a small group), you also considered your own response to Jesus' invitation. In this session you'll again be looking at John 1, this time focusing on verses 35-39. The concluding essay addresses the first step in contemplative Bible reading: the process of reading and listening to the text.

OPEN 20-30 MINUTES

Checking In

Rather than beginning this session with a sharing exercise as you have up to this point, you will start by taking no more than two minutes each to share what you have learned and heard as you have worked on the daily *lectio* experience.

❖ What are you learning about or struggling with in the *lectio* process?

❖ What do you hear from God as you work on the passage?

GROUP *LECTIO* 30-40 MINUTES

You will need three people to read the passage aloud. The leader will read the passage aloud twice, then later two different people will read. Agree on who will read the passage.

Find a comfortable place to sit—in a straight-backed chair or on the floor with your spine straight.

1. Prepare.

Ⓛ Read the following words aloud, slowly:

Sit in silence with your eyes closed. Straighten your spine, but let your body relax. Let your weight rest on the chair or the floor where you are sitting. Relax the muscles in your legs. Relax your arms. Relax your chest. Exhale deeply, and relax. Relax your throat. Relax your face. Inhale slowly, and listen to the breath as it enters your body. Listen to your breath as you breathe out.

Focus on God. If you wish, you may pray a simple prayer as you breathe in and out, such as "Lord Jesus Christ, have mercy" or "Come, Lord Jesus." We ask the Holy Spirit to speak the Word of God to us, to show us what we need to see and hear through the Scripture. As we open ourselves to the spiritual world, we ask to be surrounded and protected by God's presence. We offer to God all the concerns we have brought with us today; we lay them in God's hands so we may hear God's Word clearly.

2. Listen.

Ⓛ Say, "Listen to the Word of God. Listen for a word or phrase that touches you." Read the passage aloud, slowly:

35 The next day John was there again with two of his disciples.
36 When he saw Jesus passing by, he said, "Look, the Lamb of God!"
37 When the two disciples heard him say this, they followed
Jesus. 38 Turning around, Jesus saw them following and asked, "What do you want?"

They said, "Rabbi" (which means Teacher), "where are you staying?"

39 "Come," he replied, "and you will see."

So they went and saw where he was staying, and spent that day with him. It was about the tenth hour. (John 1:35-39)

Ⓛ After a brief pause, read the passage aloud again, slowly. Ask the group to repeat to themselves (silently) the word or phrase that touched them. Allow one minute of silence.

After the silence, say, "Let us share our words or phrases." Then share your own phrase.

Group: When it is your turn in the circle, speak your phrase aloud. Say only this word or phrase with no comments or elaboration. You may say, "I pass," at any point in this process.

3. Ask.

Ⓛ Ask, "How is my life touched by this word?"

The second reader will now read the passage aloud, slowly.

Group: Consider how your word or phrase connects to your life. Sometimes this will be an idea or a thought; at other times it will be an image or some other impression. You will have two to three minutes of silence for this meditation.

Ⓛ After two or three minutes, say, "Let us share our reflections." Then share your own thoughts on how the phrase you chose connects to your life.

Group: When it is your turn, share in one or two sentences the connection between your phrase and your life. Again, do not elaborate, explain, or justify what you sensed. One or two sentences are enough at this point.

4. Ask.

Ⓛ Ask, "Am I being invited to respond?"

The third reader now reads the passage aloud.

Group: Consider whether you are being invited to respond in some way in the next few days. Are you being encouraged to do something? You will have a few minutes of silence for meditation.

Ⓛ After two or three minutes, say, "Let us share our invitation" In one or two sentences, share the invitation you sense from the passage.

Group: When it is your turn, share in one or two sentences, without elaboration, the invitation you have received from the passage. Listen carefully to what the person on your right says because you will pray for that person based upon what he or she has shared.

5. Pray.

Ⓛ Say, "Let us pray for each other to be enabled to respond to this invitation." Pray for the person on your right.

Group: When your turn comes, pray briefly for the person on your right. If you pray silently, say, "Amen," when you finish so the next person will begin praying.

DISCUSSION 10-20 MINUTES

Use this discussion time to begin the process of group discernment. That is, talk together about what you are hearing from God. This is important. Whenever you enter into the subjective you need the balancing effect of a group of friends and fellow pilgrims who will help to affirm what you are hearing or will cause you to rethink carefully if you have misunderstood. We need others in the Christian life. To be a pilgrim following Jesus is not a solitary endeavor. We follow Jesus as part of a large band of other pilgrims: helping, encouraging, questioning, and listening to each other.

Process

1. a. Spend time discussing the step-by-step process you followed. Is any step still unclear?

   b. Which step is easiest for you?

Experience

2. a. Spend most of the time discussing the outcomes of this exercise. What are you hearing God say to you?

   b. How is this connecting with your life?

ESSAY

Step One: Reading/Listening

Lectio divina is a form of reading. It is, however, reading that focuses more on hearing than on seeing. Nowadays we read with our eyes. In fact, children are discouraged from mouthing words as they learn to read. Vocalization slows the assimilation process. But this was not the case in ancient days. Back then, to read was to speak aloud. Reading was done principally with the lips, not the eyes. Books were meant to be heard, not just seen.

In fact, meditation was understood to be the act of repeating aloud the sacred text. The Hebrew word *haga* (which is translated "meditation") means to learn the Torah by pronouncing the words in a low voice. The words were murmured aloud so as to be assimilated within.

To understand why this was the case, it is necessary to put ourselves back into the ancient world—before printing presses. Books were scarce (because they were all handwritten) and literacy was by no means universal (though by the sixth century most monks could read and write). Those who could read did so by speaking the words aloud. This aided memorization, and because you could not just pull your own copy of the Bible off the shelf and turn to a passage, it was necessary to memorize texts. Repeated vocalization of words, phrases, and passages allowed people to own the text in their hearts. A person gained a muscular and aural memory of the words, not just a visual memory. Over time, words and phrases could trigger verbal memory of whole passages, and a person recalled not only the passage but also the whole encounter with that passage before the Lord.

There is another reason for reading aloud. In an oral culture, reading aloud was a way to engage in dialogue. The text was read in order to be discussed with others. In the early church, when a letter from Paul arrived, it was read aloud to the assembled community and considered together.

Originally, *lectio divina* referred to this act of reading aloud. In the twelfth century, *lectio* was made into the four-part process we have been focusing on. But even in that process, the first step was the vocalization of sacred Scripture.

Therefore, step one in contemplative Bible reading is to read and hear the text. In group *lectio* the text is read aloud four times. In daily *lectio*, we keep going back over the text, reading it slowly over and over again to listen with full intensity. It is important to listen carefully because there is a difference between hearing and listening. We hear a lot; we listen to little. In contemplative Bible reading we need to give our full attention to the text. Short passages help such concentration—you may want to narrow your daily *lectio* to just a couple of verses. When we read, we read slowly, savoring the text, paying attention to all the words, letting the words form images in our minds.

Sometimes the text does not seem to speak to you. What you hear are words only—true words, interesting words, useful words, but not words that resonate. That, too, is fine. Repeat the text over several times until you grow familiar with it. At some later date you may be drawn back to that text. In any case, long-time practitioners of *lectio divina* counsel that there is value in the very act of hearing the Word of God—whether or not we consciously connect with the text.

What we are doing in all this is acting upon our theology. We call the Bible the Word of God. In *lectio divina* we are listening to the text as the Word of God. We are listening to God's word to us and for us and among us. In doing this we are engaging in a conversation with God.

There is one final consideration when it comes to reading and hearing the text. What text do I read? Sometimes we know what we should read. The Holy Spirit brings a passage to mind. Pay attention to such intuitions. They generally lead you to what you need to hear and reflect on. However, it is more common that we are working on a text for a particular purpose: it has been suggested by a spiritual director; it is a lectionary text; it deals with an issue with which we are wrestling; it is part of a small group we belong to (as with this series). If you are looking for texts, consult Thelma Hall's book, *Too Deep for Words*. She lists 500 *lectio* texts grouped around fifty subjects.

Daily Lectio

You may have found in your practice of daily *lectio* that your prayer and reflection do not always follow exactly the pattern for this exercise. You start off okay by reading the passage aloud. You do this several times until a word strikes you, and you reflect on it for a moment. But as you do so you remember other aspects of the passage that, in fact, interpret or amplify the word, and so you are drawn back into the text. Before you know it you are praying about several parts of the passage, not just one. Don't worry! The method is not an end in itself; it is a means to an end. Never forget that end: to know God and do God's will. As long as you remain faithful to the overall process—text-based prayer that opens your life to God—

you are accomplishing what you seek. Use the four-fold process as the basic pattern from which you start, and to which you return, in order to stay focused. Use it, but do not be confined by it.

In the week ahead, work through John 15:9-17 using the method of *lectio* outlined on pages 36-40. It is the last week of Jesus' life. He has come to Jerusalem despite warnings that he will be in great danger if he does so. It is Passover night. He has eaten the final supper he will share with the Twelve. He uses this time as a last opportunity to teach them. This is his final chance to communicate what they must know before he dies. In this poignant passage he reminds them that at the heart of his message is love. They are to love others as he loves them. He really loves them. They are not to think of themselves as servants but as his friends, special friends particularly chosen to bear rich fruit in his name.

As you read, consider carefully:

- The love of the Father
- The love of Jesus
- Loving others
- Being loved
- Being the friend of Jesus
- Being chosen
- The connection between obedience and love
- The connection between joy and love
- Bearing fruit

Session Five

The Cost of Discipleship

A Bible Study on Mark 10:17-27

Group Note: Leader's Notes for this session can be found on page 110.

Overview

Jesus had many followers beyond his team of twelve close disciples. At one point in his ministry the crowds who followed Jesus were so large that he had to stay outside the towns in isolated areas (Mark 1:45, 3:7-12). These followers included Nicodemus, a member of the Jewish ruling council who came by night; Zacchaeus, who repaid fourfold those he cheated; Mary and Martha, who were good friends (and whose story we will study in sessions seven and eight); and the rich young ruler, whose story we examine in this session. By examining how others came to Jesus, we learn how we, too, come to Jesus. In the case of this young man, we are confronted with the profound power that possessions have over us, and the challenge this is to the spiritual life.

You will open by discussing how to spend a million dollars as a fun way to think about the role of wealth in our lives. You will then study Mark 10:17-27, the encounter between Jesus and the rich young ruler.

OPEN — 20-30 MINUTES

A Million Dollars

If you had a million dollars that you had to spend on one or more causes or projects, how would you spend it?

1. I would give a million dollars to (be sure to explain your answer):

2. Now that you have given away a million dollars to worthy causes, you get to spend another million dollars on yourself! I would use a million dollars to

❏ travel
❏ buy a great house
❏ start an art collection
❏ start a retirement fund
❏ start my own business
❏ buy a farm
❏ start an auto collection
❏ retire
❏ develop a wildlife sanctuary
❏ fund my own research
❏ other:

3. Alas, you probably do not have a million dollars to give away or to spend. But you have money to donate. Which project has given you the most joy to support?

THE PASSAGE 5 MINUTES

[17]As Jesus started on his way, a man ran up to him and fell
on his knees before him. "Good teacher," he asked, "what must
I do to inherit eternal life?"
[18]"Why do you call me good?" Jesus answered. "No one is
good—except God alone. [19]You know the commandments: 'Do
not murder, do not commit adultery, do not steal, do not give
false testimony, do not defraud, honor your father and mother.'"
[20]"Teacher," he declared, "all these I have kept since I was a
boy."
[21]Jesus looked at him and loved him. "One thing you lack,"
he said. "Go, sell everything you have and give to the poor, and
you will have treasure in heaven. Then come, follow me."
[22]At this the man's face fell. He went away sad, because he
had great wealth.
[23]Jesus looked around and said to his disciples, "How hard
it is for the rich to enter the kingdom of God!"
[24]The disciples were amazed at his words. But Jesus said
again, "Children, how hard it is to enter the kingdom of God!
[25]It is easier for a camel to go through the eye of a needle than
for a rich man to enter the kingdom of God."
[26]The disciples were even more amazed, and said to each
other, "Who then can be saved?"
[27]Jesus looked at them and said, "With man this is impossible, but not with God; all things are possible with God."
(Mark 10:17-27)

ANALYSIS 10-15 MINUTES

The Young Man

4. a. Describe the young man. Who is he? What issues concern him? What type of person is he?

   b. What is the value in keeping the commandments? What is the problem in keeping the commandments?

   c. What is the problem of wealth? What is the value of wealth?

The Disciples

5. a. What amazes the disciples?

   b. What is Jesus' response to their amazement? What does he mean by these words?

Jesus

6. a. What does Jesus feel about this young man? About the Twelve? About all who would follow him?

   b. What do you learn about Jesus from this passage?

   c. What do you learn about *following* Jesus from this passage?

RESONANCE **20-30 MINUTES**

What We Love

7. a. In what ways is your story like the story of the young man?

   b. What sparked your interest in the spiritual life (eternal life)?

How We Struggle

8. a. With which of the six issues (commandments) do you struggle, if any?

   b. In what ways do you wrestle with the question of wealth: its acquisition, its maintenance, and its use?

   c. In what ways are your possessions an impediment to your spiritual life? An aid to your spiritual life?

What Jesus Says to Us

9. With what statement of Jesus do you identify the most? Explain.

   ❑ Why do you call me good?
   ❑ You know the commandments.
   ❑ I love you.
   ❑ Go sell. . . .
   ❑ Give to the poor.
   ❑ Come, follow me.
   ❑ How hard it is to enter the kingdom of God.
   ❑ All things are possible with God.

PRAYER

5-10 MINUTES

10. Let each person identify in thirty seconds or less one thing God has been saying to him or her personally through this study.

11. Go around the circle a second time and let each person pray for the small group member on his or her right, based on what that person just shared about the impact of the text.

BIBLE STUDY NOTES

Context: When Luke tells this story, he identifies this man as a ruler (a leader in the Jewish community, Luke 18:18); Matthew tells us he is young (Matthew 19:20); and all three gospel writers say he is rich. Only Mark tells us that Jesus loved him (Mark 17:21). The young man's sincerity and his feeling about Jesus are clear: he knelt, and he called Jesus "good teacher." But his commitment to his possessions is even stronger.

What Jesus asks of this young man can sound harsh and unreasonable to our ears, and we struggle to make sense of his words. We are troubled by this passage because we in North America possess so much in comparison to the rest of the world. We devote so much of our energy to securing a comfortable lifestyle. And while we are often generous with our money, we are also haunted by our need for it. But the issue in this passage is not so much wealth itself, but our attitude toward it.

Verse 17: The young man calls Jesus "good," implying that some people (presumably like Jesus and the young man himself) are moral (keep the law) and therefore deserve heaven. Jesus refuses to accept such a distinction. He has just said to his disciples (in verses 14-15) that to enter the kingdom of God we must become like little children—like children in their openness and dependence. The kingdom is received by faith. In contrast, the young man wants to know what to do. He does not yet understand that salvation is a gift to be received, not a reward to be earned.

The question is not so much whether we have good feelings toward Jesus, but whether we will follow him. On what basis do you come to Jesus? What question do you have for Jesus as you start (or restart) your spiritual pilgrimage?

Verses 18-20: No one can claim to be good because only God is good. Jesus cuts to the heart of the young man's problem: equating being good with gaining eternal life. The insecurity of such a position is demonstrated in the young man's need to ask if he has eternal life even though he has really tried to be good.

Jesus refers to six of the ten commandments, the ones that deal with our relationships with other people. The young ruler is apparently sincere in asserting that he has kept all these; Jesus does not dispute his claim to have done so. What he missed is Jesus' insistence (in the Sermon on the Mount, for example) that law-keeping involves inner attitudes as well as outer actions. At this level we all fail.

Even when we know that God's acceptance of us is "by grace through faith," we act as if it depends upon our efforts. On the other hand, to say, "I trust Jesus for my salvation," and then live without regard to any of his teachings is a contradiction and makes our profession of faith suspect. The call is to trust Christ and to love him by living as he would live.

Verses 21-22: Before Jesus, riches were not considered a hindrance to spiritual pursuit. In fact, wealth was thought to be a sign of God's blessing (see Job 1:10, 42:10; Psalm 128:1-2; Isaiah 3:10). But here Jesus points out that wealth can hinder participation in God's kingdom. Possessions are this man's problem, so Jesus tells him to get rid of them. Jesus contrasts treasure on earth (which the man has) with treasure in heaven (which he wants). The young man professes an interest in the one but, when pressed, will not give up the other. Jesus' words do not appear to be a universal prohibition against wealth. The primary call to this young man is not to follow poverty but to follow Jesus. However, it is a strong warning about the negative power of possessions.

The rich man turns away. The demand is too great. He refuses the call to follow Jesus. By walking away he demonstrates

Jesus' point: wealth can be a snare preventing us from discipleship. There is a sadness to this story both in the young man (his face fell) and in Jesus (who loved him and who comments wistfully on the power of riches over people).

When St. Anthony (born in A.D. 251) heard these words: "Go, sell everything . . . follow me," he understood them to be a personal call from God. He withdrew into the desert for a life of solitude. When he emerged twenty years later, the crowds flocked to him because they recognized in him the holiness of life. St. Anthony is considered to be the father of the monastic movement.

Jesus' words, "One thing you lack . . ." pinpoint the issue that impedes the young man from following of Jesus. What issue in your life hinders you from following Jesus?

Verses 23-25: The camel was the largest animal in Israel, and a needle had the smallest opening. Thus the absolute impossibility of anyone (the reference to the rich is dropped here) entering the kingdom of God through his or her own efforts.

Wealth is the issue in North America today. So much time and energy is given to its accumulation. So much evil is justified by its acquisition. So much pain is caused by its pursuit. It is very hard for North Americans to get the balance right between money as a good gift from God and the love of money as the root of all kinds of evil (as the apostle Paul says). How does the desire for money affect you?

Verses 26-27: Jesus responds to the disciples' fear. Eternal life cannot be earned by men and women, but it will be given by God. We are all dependent upon God and must rest in the good pleasure of a good God who loves us.

The call is to rest in the love of the God of the impossible. Are you resting in that love?

Session Six

The Cost of Discipleship

A *Lectio* Exercise on Mark 10:23,27

Group Note:
Leader's Notes for this session can be found on page 110.

Overview

In the "Checking In" exercise for this session you will share insights from your experience with daily *lectio*. Then you will use Mark 10:23,27 for your *lectio* exercise. The concluding essay focuses on the second step in contemplative Bible reading: the process of meditation.

OPEN 20-30 MINUTES

Checking In

Begin by checking in with each other. Take up to two minutes per person to share what you have been learning and hearing as you have worked on the daily *lectio* experience. When it comes to experiential exercises such as *lectio*, it is very important to process your experience with others.

GROUP *LECTIO* 30-40 MINUTES

Because you are becoming familiar with the group *lectio* process, the steps are only summarized in this session. If you wish, you may refer to the full instructions in session two (pages 31-40). The passage you will use is a compilation of Jesus' words in Mark 10:23,27.

Decide who will read the passage each time. Then be sure to spend enough time preparing for the experience. Take time to get in touch with God by doing the centering exercise.

1. *Prepare:* Relax, slow your breathing, use a centering prayer if you wish. Ask the Holy Spirit to speak to you.

2. *Listen:* Read the passage aloud twice. After one minute, share your word or phrase.

   Jesus . . . said to his disciples, "How hard it is for the rich to enter the kingdom of God! . . . With man this is impossible, but not with God; all things are possible with God." (Mark 10:23,27)

3. *Ask:* "How is my life touched by this word?" Read the passage aloud. After two or three minutes, share your reflections.

4. *Ask:* "Am I being invited to respond?" Read the passage aloud. After two or three minutes, share the invitation you sense.

5. *Pray:* Pray for the person on your right, for the ability to respond to his or her invitation.

DISCUSSION 10-20 MINUTES

By now the process of contemplative Bible reading should be familiar to you. Use this time to discuss what you are hearing God say to you—both from today's exercise and from the other *lectio* experiences. Become "friendly ears" for each another; helping each other with the struggle to know and do God's will. Also be alert to what does not sound like it comes from God. In a discipline such as contemplative Bible reading, it is essential to offer our "hearing" up to others' scrutiny and to process it with them, trusting in the wisdom of the gathered community. Our compulsions and our history sometimes get in the way of hearing God accurately, and the community can help us recognize this.

Ponder what God is saying to people in the group. Listen to one another. Discern together. Support one another.

ESSAY

Step Two: Meditation

Meditation is a key spiritual exercise. It lies at the heart of *lectio divina*. Meditation is not an esoteric art as it is sometimes thought to be. In fact, it's quite natural. It's something we engage in all the time though we may not call it by that name. To meditate is to think about a subject. It is to focus on a topic, turning it over in your mind until it becomes clear or until you have new insight. Meditation is a form of reflection; it is a way of learning. Meditation is rumination, the use of imagination to gain new insight.

What sets meditation apart (in the sense that we use it here) from everyday rumination is the subject matter. Meditation focuses on spiritual matters: the meaning of a particular verse, how to deal with a present temptation, the sense of God's presence, and so on. *To meditate is to make use of a natural skill for a spiritual purpose.*

To meditate is to give free rein to our imagination in order to grasp what God is saying to us in Scripture. In *lectio divina*, we are invited to "see" the passage, that is, to imagine what is happening: to see how people dress, to hear the conversation, to notice the color, to feel the breeze, to smell the wood smoke, to watch the motion of the crowds. We listen to Jesus speaking (rather than just read his words). In this way we are open to the experience of God's love and not just the knowledge that God loves us. Using our imagination in Bible study is a powerful way to encounter the text.

It needs to be added that some people are more adept at using their imagination in this way than others. If this form of meditation works for you, by all means use it. If not, don't worry. There are other forms of prayer appropriate for you.[1] For example, you may find it a powerful experience simply to repeat Jesus' words from the text, letting them sink into your soul. Or meditation may mean for you to write the phrase you are focusing on in your journal, then put down related thoughts or try to summarize what that phrase means to you. This, too, is a form of meditation.

There is a second distinction that can be made between meditation and ordinary reflection. Meditation is not just a question of subject matter. It is also a question of outcome. To meditate is to think about a subject in order to do it. It is to practice a thing by thinking about it. It is to desire it in your mind even as you seek to express it in your life. In other words, this is not idle rumination, but rumination with a purpose. To meditate on a text is to understand that text so deeply that you live it out. It is to incorporate a concept into your everyday existence. This is why meditation is so valuable as a spiritual practice. It is a way of translating the Bible into life.

But I find more in meditation than just connections to my life. I also learn more about God. I am struck by a variety of things concerning who God is or what God is saying about himself. I feel drawn to God in a certain way. I experience the presence of God or the love of God or the peace of God as I meditate. Therefore, meditation is not just a means of doing, but also a means of being.

Daily Lectio

In the week ahead, work through Matthew 11:25-30 using the *lectio divina* method. This passage consists of three parts: a prayer of thanksgiving, a wise utterance, and an invitation from Jesus.

The passage begins with a prayer of Jesus. Throughout the Gospels we hear that Jesus has prayed or is praying, and we read some of his prayers.[2] That prayer stood at the center of Jesus' spiritual life is the strongest possible indication that prayer should be at the heart of our spiritual life. *Lectio* is a process of prayer.

After his prayer, Jesus comments on how the spiritual life functions. We are totally dependent upon God's grace. Salvation may be impossible for us to achieve on our own, but with God all things are possible.

This passage ends with a warm and gracious invitation to us in our weariness. Jesus calls us to himself. This is not a call to passivity or inaction. We are invited to take upon ourselves a "yoke." But this is not like the yoke of the law which weighs down and binds us. This is a yoke of gentleness and humility, of discipleship. It means to be bound together with Jesus in our pilgrimage.

The central image here is a yoke. This may refer to the kind of yoke that linked two oxen together to pull a plow, or it may be the yoke placed by the victor on his captives to parade them through town. Regardless, the image is clear: we are bound by this yoke together with Jesus. But this is not a burdensome binding. Jesus' yoke is easy (because he is pulling most of the weight) and his burden is light (unlike the weight of the Law the Pharisees placed on people). This is the yoke that enlivens, not the yoke that deadens.

Notes

1. See Chester Michael and Marie Norrisey, *Prayer and Temperament: Different Prayer Forms for Different Personality Types* (Charlottesville, VA: The Open Door, 1984).
2. For more information on the prayer life of Jesus read William David Spencer and Aída Besançon Spencer, *The Prayer Life of Jesus: Shout of Agony, Revelation of Love* (Lanham, MD: University Press of America, 1991).

Session Seven

The Priorities of Life

A Bible Study on Luke 10:38-42

> **Group Note:**
> Leader's Notes for this session can be found on page 110.

Overview

Many women followed Jesus as his disciples and his friends. This was unusual in the first century, when women were considered to be mere property with few rights of their own. They were not seen as independent individuals who would make fit disciples. However, Jesus refused to be bound by these social conventions. He treated women as equals. He welcomed them as his followers in the same way he welcomed men.

In the passage we are studying, Mary and Martha are clearly more than disciples; they are friends of Jesus. There is a light, comfortable feeling to this scene. One can picture Jesus relaxing in his or her home, not pressed by the crowds wanting something from him, but in conversation with old friends about issues that matter. In their dialogue we are confronted with our need to balance work with the rest of life and to discern what really matters in life.

To begin this session, you will get to explore your personality "type." This will be good preparation for understanding the encounter between Martha and her quite different sister Mary, which you will study in Luke 10:38-42. As you study this passage you will consider your priorities in life as you follow Jesus.

OPEN 20-30 MINUTES

What's Your Type?

The Myers-Briggs Type Indicator (MBTI)[1] is a widely used personality test that can help you better understand yourself and the others in the group. We cannot provide the MBTI test, much less take the time to score it and explore it. But you can make a good first guess at the four letters that identify your type.

1. What is your type? In each of the four categories, circle the preference that most closely fits who you are. Don't worry if the fit is only approximate.

   a. Are you an Introvert (I) or an Extrovert (E)? Circle I or E.

   ❑ An Introvert gets new energy by being alone; reflects on what he/she thinks before speaking; is a good listener; likes being with a few good friends; finds socializing to be draining after a while.

   ❑ An Extrovert gets new energy from being with other people; figures out what he/she thinks by talking it out; is a great conversationalist; likes parties; works best in the company of others.

   b. Do you gather data through Sensing (S) or Intuition (N)? Circle S or N.

   ❑ A Sensor prefers specific answers to specific questions; likes jobs with visible results; works with facts rather than theories; likes clear instructions; is a literalist; focuses on the specific.

   ❑ An Intuitive juggles several thoughts simultaneously; gets excited about future possibilities; finds details boring; likes the big picture; loves puns; sees interrelationships between things.

c. Do you make decisions by Thinking (T) or Feeling (F)? (Warning: do not interpret "feeling" here to mean "emotional.") Circle T or F.

❏ A Thinker makes decisions based on what is objective, logical, and true; prefers to be right rather than liked; is calm in conflict; likes to argue in a discussion.

❏ A Feeler makes decisions that take into account the feelings of others; senses what others are experiencing and feeling; makes decisions on the basis of values; prefers harmony to clarity; takes things personally; accommodates others.

d. Do you respond in a Judging (J) or Perceiving (P) way? (Warning: don't try to understand these terms in their normal senses!) Circle J or P.

❏ A Judger is on time; is organized; knows what others should be doing; hates surprises; makes schedules; plans ahead.

❏ A Perceiver has trouble with deadlines; is spontaneous; likes to keep options open; loves the unknown; responds to the moment; is flexible.[2]

2. Go around the group and share your type. Then

a. let one I and one E talk about what energizes them,
b. let one S and one N talk about the role of details in life,
c. let one T and one F talk about how to make decisions, and
d. let one J and one P talk about organizing a small group session.

3. Compare the types of those in your group who find contemplative Bible reading easy and exhilarating, and the types of those who find it difficult and stressful. Do you see any connections between type and preferred spiritual style?

THE PASSAGE **5 MINUTES**

38As Jesus and his disciples were on their way, he came to a village where a woman named Martha opened her home to him.
39She had a sister called Mary, who sat at the Lord's feet listening to what he said. 40But Martha was distracted by all the
preparations that had to be made. She came to him and asked,
"Lord, don't you care that my sister has left me to do the work
by myself? Tell her to help me!"
41"Martha, Martha," the Lord answered, "you are worried
and upset about many things, 42but only one thing is needed.
Mary has chosen what is better, and it will not be taken away
from her." (Luke 10:38-42)

ANALYSIS **10-15 MINUTES**

Jesus and Mary

4. a. What do you know about Mary from this passage? What kind of person is she?

   b. Who do you know like Mary? What are that person's strengths and weaknesses?

   c. Why does Jesus commend Mary? How do you feel about this given the situation?

Jesus and Martha

5. a. What do you know about Martha from this passage? What kind of person is she?

   b. Who do you know like Martha? What are that person's strengths and weaknesses?

   c. What impact, do you suppose, did her complaint about Mary have on the dinner party?

d. Why does Jesus respond as he does to Martha? How do you feel about his response given the situation?

6. What does Jesus mean when he says "only one thing is needed"?

RESONANCE **20-30 MINUTES**

7. Rate the following activities according to how important they are to you, beginning with (1) for the most important:

____ job	____ conversation
____ study	____ childcare
____ tasks	____ relationships
____ church	____ sleeping
____ eating	____ spiritual disciplines
____ reading	____ other:
____ leisure	

8. Go back over this list and indicate how much time you actually spend per day on each activity. What discrepancies, if any, are there between what you value and how you spend your time?

9. Are you most like Mary or Martha in the following areas?

a. work	❏ Mary	❏ Martha
b. relationships	❏ Mary	❏ Martha
c. responsibility	❏ Mary	❏ Martha
d. time management	❏ Mary	❏ Martha
e. spiritual discipline	❏ Mary	❏ Martha

10. What have you determined is the "one thing needed" in your life after all this conversation and analysis?

PRAYER 5-10 MINUTES

11. Let each person identify in thirty seconds or less one thing God has been saying to him or her personally through this study.

12. Go around the circle a second time and let each person pray for the small group member on his or her right, based on what that person just shared about the impact of the text.

BIBLE STUDY NOTES

Context: Luke is the only Gospel writer who tells us this wonderful story. However, you can get a fuller sense of Mary and Martha by reading John 11:1–12:10. Clearly, Martha is a strong and forceful woman with a quick mind, able to hold her own with Jesus. Mary is more in touch with her feelings and more naturally relational. John identifies her as the woman who poured expensive perfume on Jesus' feet in anticipation of his burial and then wiped it off with her hair (an act that would have shocked onlookers because women did not unbind their hair in public). John also tells us that Jesus loved Mary, Martha, and their brother Lazarus (John 11:5).

Verse 38: Jesus was traveling with his disciples (probably the Twelve though more may have been included). The singular pronouns ("he came to a village" and "Martha opened her home to him") may indicate that he alone stopped there. On the other hand, it may have been that thirteen people stopped by, in which case Martha's frantic preparation is better understood. From John 11 it's clear that this home was a place Jesus knew and was comfortable in, the home of good friends.

Verse 39: With these few words (plus Martha's comments in verse 40), Luke describes Mary to us. In Myers-Briggs language, Mary is a P. She responds to the moment. She would rather engage in conversation than plan a meal. She is probably fun to be with, though you would not want her to organize your finances or do your taxes. She is adaptable, flexible, relational, and spontaneous, but she is neither goal-oriented nor an organizer.

Jesus encourages Mary in her eagerness to learn. His response would have put him at odds with the prevailing notion of the time that Jewish teachers, for the most part, did not view women as learners. In fact, Johanan of Jerusalem gave this advice: "Talk not much with womenkind." Another rabbi said, "If any man gives his daughter knowledge of the Law, it is as though he taught her lechery."

Mary is a disciple. She wants to learn from Jesus. She chooses the kind of active reflection that goes on between teacher and student. *Lectio* is a way to attend to the Word of God and let it affect us.

Verse 40: Martha is distracted by the need to make preparations. It seems that she, too, wants to learn, but the pressures of hospitality prevent that. She is annoyed that Mary is not helping. She also may be annoyed that Jesus is encouraging this behavior and that she has to feed a crowd (if the disciples are there).

If Mary is a P, Martha is a J. A J needs control over life and so organizes, plans, and puts a lot of energy into making things go smoothly. Js don't like surprises, get irritated when other people don't do things right, have a schedule, and thrive on order. Js can drive you crazy, but they get things done.

What role does work play in your life? While the evidence is too slim to label Martha a workaholic, it is clear that in her preoccupation with preparing a meal for her guest, she is willing and able to work hard. The issue is not just work (somebody had to fix the meal), but choices (could she have prepared a simpler meal or waited to fix dinner until a lull in the conversation?). How do we choose to use our time? Are our choices always the best? Does it really need to get done? Does activity (work) play far too large a role in our lives?

A second issue is tension between siblings. Most of us know this scene firsthand. There is work to be done. One sibling gets stuck with it, and the other won't help. There is anger between the two. An appeal is made to a third party. What tension do you live with (or have you lived with) regarding siblings or with your children and their relationships?

Verses 41-42: Jesus' affection for Martha comes out in his reply "Martha, Martha. . . ." He invites her to calm down. Then he describes her situation. She is "fretting and fussing about so many things" as the *New English Bible* translates the phrase. The challenge for her is to step back from the pressures of the moment and think about the larger issues.

What do you fret and fuss about? Maybe you don't fret and fuss at all, so things never get done. Jesus challenges us to fit our concerns and preoccupations into larger realities. Is all our activity necessary? How has all this activity made us feel? Is it worth it?

Certainly, Mary's choice to listen to Jesus is the better way here. This story is sometimes used to promote the contemplative way above the activist path, but this is not the issue. Clearly both modes are needed in the spiritual life. The question here is one of priorities.

Notes

1. For more information on the Myers-Briggs Type Indicator see David Keirsey and Marilyn Bates, *Please Understand Me: Character and Temperament Types* (Del Mar, CA: Prometheus/Nemesis Book Company, 1989).
2. This way of talking about type is based on *Type Talk* by Otto Kroeger and Janet Thuesen (Delacorte Press) as described in Roy M. Oswald and Otto Kroeger, *Personality Type and Religious Leadership* (Bethesda, MD: Alban Institute, 1988).

Session Eight

The Priorities of Life

A *Lectio* Exercise on Luke 10:41-42

Group Note:
Leader's Notes for this session are not required.

Overview

In session seven you took a closer look at Luke 10:38-42, which showcased two of Jesus' friends, Mary and Martha. By exploring how these two women interacted with Jesus during a social visit, you gained an introductory insight into how your own personality type might influence your encounters with Jesus.

For your *lectio* exercise in this session you will reflect on a compilation of Jesus' words in Luke 10:41-42, the same passage you studied in session seven. The concluding essay discusses the third step in contemplative Bible reading: prayer.

OPEN 20-30 MINUTES

Checking In

Take up to two minutes to share what you have been learning and hearing as you have worked on the daily *lectio* experience. By now the newness of the process has worn off, and daily *lectio* now has a sense of "spiritual discipline" to it. When this way of reading and praying has become second nature, its work can reach deep inside of us. Sharing can focus on

- where you are in your mastery and use of the *lectio* process,
- the impact contemplative Bible reading is having on your spiritual life, and
- what you are hearing from God.

GROUP *LECTIO* 30-40 MINUTES

Because you are becoming familiar with the group *lectio* process, the steps are only summarized in this session. If you wish, you may refer to the full instructions in session two (pages 31-40). The passage you will use is a compilation of Jesus' words in Luke 10:41-42.

Decide who will read the passage each time. Then be sure to spend enough time preparing for the experience. Take time to get in touch with God by doing the centering exercise.

1. *Prepare:* Relax, slow your breathing, use a centering prayer if you wish. Ask the Holy Spirit to speak to you.

2. *Listen:* Read the passage aloud twice.

   "Martha, Martha," the Lord answered, "you are worried and upset about many things, but only one thing is needed. Mary has chosen what is better, and it will not be taken away from her." (Luke 10:41-42)

   After one minute, share your word or phrase.

3. *Ask:* "How is my life touched by this word?" Read the passage aloud. After two or three minutes, share your reflections.

4. *Ask:* "Am I being invited to respond?" Read the passage aloud. After two or three minutes, share the invitation you sense.

5. *Pray:* Pray for the person on your right, for the ability to respond to his or her invitation.

DISCUSSION 10-20 MINUTES

Norvene Vest says there are four practices that help to make Christ the center of your small group community:

- Speaking the truth in love
- Admitting strong emotions
- Listening in love
- Confidentiality

Discuss how well you are doing in each of these areas in your group. Continue your discussion of the group *lectio* experience.

ESSAY

Step Three: Prayer

Although step three is defined as "prayer," you have already been praying in the *lectio* experience. You began the entire process by praying. You prayed that the Holy Spirit would guide you and be present with you. You prayed as you read over the passage, listening to God's word to you. You prayed as you meditated, asking God for insight into how the text connects with your life. At first glance, it would seem strange to label step three as prayer when so much prayer has already taken place. But up to this point, your prayer has largely been an exercise of the intellect and imagination. In this step you move into "prayer of the heart."

This is not prayer for which many guidelines can be given. It is prayer that we learn as we listen to God, as we open ourselves to God.

Such prayer is not always a comfortable experience. While there is great consolation in prayer, great affirmation, and great love, there is also an underlying tension. Jesus simply will not let us remain in our false selves or pursue destructive tracks even though they may appear attractive to us. We are not just consoled in prayer, we also are confronted.

In prayer we are not simply engaging in some kind of inner psychological dialogue—talking to ourselves, as it were. Theodor Bovet, a highly regarded Swiss physician and psychiatrist, writes of this effect.

> When we think about Christ and call on him, it is not as though we were appealing to a dead or an absent person and deliberating about him: Christ answers, he has an effect on us, he is with us, he is alive. This is demonstrated in the fact that his will confronts us with increasing clarity as an absolute, complete, indeed foreign, will, radically different from our own wills. In those moments when we begin to consider Christ, we usually would like to find in him the confirmation of our own personal will, that is to say his plan should bring ours to the highest degree of perfection. But his will emerges in an entirely different context, with a completely new viewpoint, in contrast to which our will appears to be permeated with trivialities and self-seeking motives. . . .
>
> The abrupt antithesis of Christ's will to ours surprises us; we are vexed by this Otherness. . . . It can honestly be said that the characteristic of a genuine encounter with Christ is that our initial reaction is to be offended, and have nothing more to do with him. . . .
>
> Here God lays hold of our innermost self. Christ desires that I should tell the definite facts of illness to a patient [in giving this personal illustration Bovet focuses on his role as a doctor]; I resist this because I do not wish to be altogether truthful with this person. Christ would enjoin me not to attend a certain movie, for I would like to attend it chiefly

> for the purpose of arousing licentious feelings. . . . Christ thrusts me continually in to the presence of a certain person; I wish always to evade him because I do not like him and cannot forgive him. Right at this point I need to be changed.[1]

In his book *Seeking the Face of God*, William Shannon compares this type of prayer to "falling into the hands of God."[2] When we read Scripture and meditate on it, we fall into the orbit of God. We experience purification; elements of our false self are revealed and we are moved to let go of them. We also fall into the plan of God, finding our part in it. Finally, we fall into the love of God, knowing God as God really is. This is a potent type of prayer.

This is the goal of step three: deep prayer of the heart. This is not always the experience we have of prayer when we do *lectio*. At times we resist what we hear about our false self. We harden our hearts. We stop the process. At other times we are distracted. We move away from the intensity of this sort of prayer. We may not be ready for it. We may need more time in order to pray in this fashion. In the end, it is God who gives us prayer. We may need to focus on hearing God's Word and meditating on it. Our prayer is really an extension of or a summing up of what we have heard and meditated upon. We pray to act upon what we have heard. This is more than adequate. We need to rest comfortably in whatever kind of prayer God gives us.

Daily Lectio

In the week ahead work through John 4:4-26, the story of Jesus' meeting with the woman at the well.

To understand the impact of this conversation, it is necessary to know something about the religious, legal, and social situation of the Samaritan woman. In those days, this woman would have been marginalized because of her gender, race, and social status. As a woman, she was a second-class citizen. In one prayer, men actually thanked God that they had not been born women! As a Samaritan, she was viewed with suspicion because Samaritans were not descended from one of the twelve tribes of Israel (even though they claimed to be). As a woman divorced many times, she was suspect. Under the law of that time there was no limit on the number of marriages (or divorces), but only men were granted a divorce. More than three marriages was seen as very bad. For her to be living with a man to whom she was not married made her a threat to other women (which probably explains why she came alone in the heat of the day for water).

Jesus will have none of this. He actually initiates the conversation with her in a time most teachers would not talk to a strange woman. Jesus treats her with respect. In verse 21 he calls her "woman," which was a term of respect and affection (the same term Jesus used for his mother at the wedding at Cana). Furthermore, Jesus treats her as an equal, as an independent adult created in the image of God. He teaches her. He dialogues with her. He reveals to her who he is.

But it is what Jesus offers that gives this passage significance: living water. Living water was a gift from God, the gift of the Holy Spirit. Jesus not only offered living water, he claimed that it would banish thirst forever. Only the Messiah could offer that type of water. He offers this same living water to us.

Work through this passage using the *lectio divina* method of study and prayer.

Notes

1. Theodor Bovet, *Have Time and Be Free* (London: S.P.C.K., 1965), pages 29-32.
2. William Shannon, *Seeking the Face of God* (New York: Crossroads, 1990), page 94.

Session Nine

The Courage of Faith

A Bible Study on Matthew 14:22-32

Group Note:
Leader's Notes for this session can be found on page 111.

Overview

Peter was perhaps the most famous of Jesus' disciples. Early on, Peter emerged as the leader of the Twelve. He was a prominent figure in the original Jerusalem church. His story dominates the first half of Acts. He wrote two letters that appear in the New Testament. He is the voice behind the Gospel account written by Mark.

Many people identify with Peter. We like him not because of his accomplishments but because he is so human. Not a suave and politic individual, Peter always seems to be putting his foot into it. Not a high-powered executive type, Peter is a blue-collar fisherman. Not an educated man, Peter relies on others to put his words into print. He is a man of action who does not always plan ahead. In other words, Peter seems to make the same errors we make. He seems to have the same confusion we have. But in all this ordinariness, his great redeeming feature is his capacity for love and loyalty. He is loved by Jesus and responds by giving Jesus his whole life.

We learn a lot about discipleship from Peter, not only when he gets it right, but when he does it wrong. In the story for this session we see both sides of Peter: impetuous, activist, full of faith, but then overwhelmed by doubt, fearful and courageous. His story challenges us to a kind of wild, improbable faith, to step into the sort of future we would only attempt because Jesus is calling us to do so.

In the opening exercise for this session you will recall great adventures you have had as a way to imagine what it must have been like for Peter when he walked on water (Matthew 14:22-32). This passage challenges you to take courage, to keep your eyes on Jesus, to have faith not doubt, and thus to do what you could never do on your own.

OPEN 20-30 MINUTES

Adventures

What is the most amazing thing you have ever done? Maybe it was not walking on water (as Peter does in the story you will study), but for you it was remarkable. When we remember what we did in the past, we are empowered to stride boldly into the future.

1. What is the most amazing thing you have ever done? Explain.

   ❑ an adventure (traveled to China, climbed a mountain, entered an Iron Man/Woman competition)
   ❑ a challenge (left a job, started a business, overcame an illness)
   ❑ a relationship (got married, had children, made it on your own)
   ❑ a ministry (taught junior-high Sunday school, worked with AIDS patients, started a prayer group)
   ❑ a pilgrimage (became a Christian, got a spiritual director, joined an inner-city mission)
   ❑ other:

2. What made it possible for you to do this?

3. What is the challenge you are facing at this point in your life? You are being called to. . .

❑ move	❑ grow	❑ change
❑ hang in there	❑ hope	❑ believe
❑ pull back	❑ step in	❑ love
❑ stop	❑ step out	❑ start
❑ step forward	❑ step back	❑ other:

THE PASSAGE 5 MINUTES

[22]Immediately Jesus made the disciples get into the boat and go on ahead of him to the other side, while he dismissed the crowd. [23]After he had dismissed them, he went up on a mountainside by himself to pray. When evening came, he was there alone, [24]but the boat was already a considerable distance from land, buffeted by the waves because the wind was against it.

[25]During the fourth watch of the night Jesus went out to them, walking on the lake. [26]When the disciples saw him walking on the lake, they were terrified. "It's a ghost," they said, and cried out in fear.

[27]But Jesus immediately said to them: "Take courage! It is I. Don't be afraid."

[28]"Lord, if it's you," Peter replied, "tell me to come to you on the water."

[29]"Come," he said.

Then Peter got down out of the boat, walked on the water and came toward Jesus. [30]But when he saw the wind, he was afraid and, beginning to sink, cried out, "Lord, save me!"

[31]Immediately Jesus reached out his hand and caught him. "You of little faith," he said, "why did you doubt?"

[32]And when they climbed into the boat, the wind died down. [33]Then those who were in the boat worshiped him, saying, "Truly you are the Son of God." (Matthew 14:22-33)

ANALYSIS 10-15 MINUTES

Today's questions are a little different from what you are used to. They ask you to imagine. Use the data from the text in order to see, hear, and feel what this situation must have been like for the disciples, especially Peter. This is an exercise in imaginative meditation.

The Disciples (Verses 22-27)

4. a. Imagine what it must have been like for the disciples to be ushered into their boat after the feeding of the five thousand and sent out onto the lake to battle for their lives against the wind. Then they see a ghost walking across the water—and it turns out to be Jesus! As you try to take all this in, what are your impressions of the sights, sounds, smells, thoughts, and emotions of that scene?

   b. What were the disciples feeling about Jesus in all this?

Peter (Verses 28-33)

5. a. Imagine what it must have been like for Peter when Jesus invited him to walk on water. What made him do that? What was Peter thinking and feeling when he made his wild request, when he heard Jesus call him to come, when he actually took that first step onto the water, when his single-minded focus on Jesus began to waver and he noticed the wind and waves, when he began to sink, when he cried out to Jesus, when he got back into the boat? What are your impressions of the sights, sounds, smells, thoughts, and emotions of that scene?

   b. What did the disciples learn about Jesus through Peter's experience?

RESONANCE 20-30 MINUTES

6. What unbelievable feat have you attempted in the past simply because Jesus called you to do it?

7. What is the name of the fear that has the power to cause you to sink?

8. What act of faith is Jesus now calling you to undertake?

PRAYER 5-10 MINUTES

9. Let everyone identify in thirty seconds or less one thing God has been saying to him or her personally through this study.

10. Go around the circle a second time and let each person pray for the small group member on his or her right, based on what that person just shared about the impact of the text.

BIBLE STUDY NOTES

Context: Jesus has just fed five thousand people. The crowds are enthusiastic, to say the least. John tells us that they wanted to take Jesus and "make him king by force" (John 6:15). The situation is volatile. It could erupt into an ill-formed, ill-conceived peasant revolt that is sure to end in bloodshed. Jesus defuses the situation by sending his disciples off to the lake in their boat and withdrawing somehow into the hills. He then reconnects with the disciples in this somewhat unorthodox fashion.

The themes of this passage are storm, stress, fear, faith, doubt, and worship. In other words, it is a rich passage filled with issues that we too must face as we live the life of faith.

Verses 22-24: Jesus gives the disciples no option. He "compels" them (this is the force of the verb translated "made") to leave in the boat. Jesus' response to the situation is to withdraw on his own and pray. The disciples, on the other hand, are having a rough time of it, battling against a strong head wind.

Are we influenced more by the heat of the moment ("Let's make Jesus king") than by listening to what God wants in a situation ("My time has not yet come")? To know God's will takes time, prayer, faith, and the wisdom of others.

Verses 25-26: Somewhere between three and six in the morning, Jesus goes out onto the lake. How he does this is not clear. That he has power over the elements had already been demonstrated when he instantly calmed the wind and the waves on this very lake (Mark 4:35-41). Even though the disciples know of his power, they are still frightened. They assume the worst. Who else but a ghost could walk on water? They feel a kind of dark terror—the sort of involuntary response we have when we encounter a supernatural being.

Our fears often drive us. Mostly we fear the unknown—"what might be." When we are afraid, we need Jesus.

Verse 27: In identifying himself, Jesus used an interesting phrase, which can be translated "It is I" but also can mean "I AM," echoing the great Old Testament name for God (Exodus 3:14; Isaiah 43:10). The disciples are afraid of a ghost when, in fact, Jesus is far greater (and more terrifying) than any mere ghost!

Verses 28-30: Peter tests whether it is actually Jesus by asking Jesus to invite him onto the lake. To Peter's credit, he comes when Jesus calls, despite how outrageous the situation is. To walk on water, who could imagine! He takes that first step on to the water. That Peter has faith enough to attempt to copy Jesus' amazing feat says a lot. That he does not succeed because he allows himself to get distracted makes him human. Notice that Peter does not attempt this seemingly impossible feat until he hears Jesus invite him to do so. Peter wavered when he "saw the wind." This probably means when he sees the effect of the wind on the water, whipping up waves.

Verse 31: In contrast to Peter's great faith (what must it have been like to take that first step onto the water?) is Peter's little faith that results in his sinking (how terrifying to feel yourself go down into the dark, wild water). The contrast in this passage is not between belief and disbelief, but between belief and inadequate belief. Jesus uses the word "doubt" to describe Peter's state of mind. This is a word that means "in two minds" or "divided in two." The contrast is between having a single-minded focus on Jesus (and thus being able to act courageously and do the impossible) and having a focus divided between Jesus and the wind that threatens to overwhelm.

Verses 32-33: When Peter and Jesus return to the boat, the wind dies down. The emergency is over. The disciples' response to all this is worship and praise. Peter has moved from stress (the hard work of sailing the boat into the wind) to fear (of a ghost) to courage (when Jesus reveals himself and Peter asks to come to him) to faith (he walks on water) to doubt (he sinks) to fear again ("save me") to worship—all this in a matter of moments! In simple terms, this is the Christian walk: the stress of life, the fear of many things, the courage that comes in the discovery of Jesus, the faith in Jesus that leads us to step out in new ways, the doubts that assail us as we move forward, the fear that returns, the need to reach out again to Jesus, and the worship when we discover anew his sustaining power—all this in a matter of a lifetime!

Session Ten

The Courage of Faith

A *Lectio* Exercise on Matthew 14:27-29

Group Note:
Leader's Notes for this session can be found on page 111.

Overview

In session nine we looked at an incident from Matthew 14:22-32, showing the apostle Peter responding to Jesus with impetuousness, action, faith, doubt, fear, and courage. It is a moving account, and it challenges us to a kind of wild, improbable faith, to step into the sort of future we would only attempt because Jesus is calling us to do so.

In this session you will again look at Peter's story in Matthew 14, this time focusing on verses 27-29, in which Jesus invites Peter to step out and do the impossible. The focus of the concluding essay is on the fourth step in contemplative Bible reading: contemplation.

GROUP *LECTIO* — 30-40 MINUTES

The passage you will use for this exercise is the dialogue between Peter and Jesus (Matthew 14:27-29). Decide who will read the passage each time. Then get in touch with God by doing the centering exercise.

1. *Prepare:* Relax, slow your breathing, use a centering prayer if you wish. Ask the Holy Spirit to speak to you.

2. *Listen:* Read the passage aloud twice.

   Jesus immediately said to them: "Take courage! It is I. Don't be afraid."

   "Lord, if it's you," Peter replied, "tell me to come to you on the water."

   "Come," he said.

   Then Peter got down out of the boat, walked on the water and came toward Jesus. (Matthew 14:27-29)

   After one minute, share your word or phrase.

3. *Ask:* "How is my life touched by this word?" Read the passage aloud. After two or three minutes, share your reflections.

4. *Ask:* "Am I being invited to respond?" Read the passage aloud. After two or three minutes, share the invitation you sense.

5. *Pray:* Pray for the person on your right, for the ability to respond to this invitation.

DISCUSSION 10-20 MINUTES

Summarize your experience of the *lectio divina* process. Was it easy or difficult? Useful or not so useful? How do you intend to use this process now that the group is ending? What is one key thing you have heard from God during this experience?

FAREWELL **20-30 MINUTES**

Discuss the next step for your group. Here are a few possibilities.

- *Spiritual Formation series*: Take a short break (two weeks) and then start up again. Work on another spiritual discipline. Consider *Meditative Prayer: Entering God's Presence*, in which you will learn various ways to pray. This is a natural follow-up to the *lectio* style of prayer you have been practicing. The other topics in this series are spiritual journaling and spiritual autobiography. (An additional option would be *Listening to God: Using Scripture as a Path to God's Presence* by Jan Johnson.)

- *Bible study*: You might want to continue as a group but switch to Bible study.

- *Retreat*: Go on a retreat together. Most locales have retreat centers that offer silent or guided retreats. This is a great way to deepen your relationship with God.

- *Multiply*: If this has been a meaningful experience for you, why not start other contemplative Bible reading groups? Work as a team and recruit new members. Help others learn this way to experience Scripture.

- *Teach*: Teach the process of contemplative Bible reading in a Sunday school class or one-day seminar.

- *Conclude*: It may be time to bring this group to a close. If you do, you might want to discuss the plans for growth on the part of each member. You might also want to plan a reunion dinner scheduled in a few months.

Say good-bye to one another in a way appropriate for your group. Here are some possibilities.

- *Group prayer*: Join hands and spend time in prayer together, committing the whole experience and each person to God.

- *Affirmation*: Focus on one person at a time. Allow the other group members to express briefly what they have come to care about in that person (such as his or her courage, honesty, ability to empathize, commitment to ministry, ability to love, practical good sense, friendliness, wisdom). Then gather around that person, lay hands on him or her, and pray God's blessing on that person.

- *Liturgy*: Prepare a final liturgy using both the ancient prayers of the church and new prayers written for the group. You can plan this liturgy as a group or assign the task to one or two members. Use this as your final experience together.

ESSAY

Step Four: Contemplation

The goal of *lectio divina* is contemplation: the communication of love between God and us. This form of communication is too deep for words. Contemplation is resting prayer; it is entering into the presence of God and simply waiting. It is prayer we cannot control. It is up to God. Contemplation is being, not doing.

We tend to speak of meditation and contemplation as two words for the same thing. In fact, they are quite different. Meditation is a mental exercise. It is a natural process we use for spiritual purposes. Contemplation is a spiritual experience. It is not a natural process, nor can we conjure it up. It is a gift from God. Meditation involves the use of natural senses and faculties. Contemplation goes beyond all sense and faculty. While we know what to "do" when it comes to the first three steps in the *lectio* process, the only thing we can "do" when it comes to contemplation is simply rest in silence. It is God who does the doing.

In fact, contemplation is a form of relationship. It is the experience of being with the Beloved. It is the normal residence of those who seek the love of God.

> We have been taught as Christians, and presumably have believed, that "we are created for union with God"— but in practice we seem not to dare to accept the full

implications of this on a subjective level, to really embrace it as the central truth of our lives. Least of all, perhaps, are we prepared to trust that this is God's passionate desire for us. (How frustrating, for the Lover!)

At best, perhaps, we vaguely accept that somehow, somewhere, "in heaven," we will come to this union of love. But Jesus' life and teachings concern our lives here and now: "The kingdom of heaven is within you". . . . "Repent, and believe the good news": you are beloved of God! His message is that we love him in loving one another, and that love is the love of God, living and loving through us in this world, as its source, meaning, and end.

It is this love which becomes experiential in contemplative prayer, and gradually informs our lives to become more and more a presence of God's love in the world.[1]

In the end, contemplation is about awareness—awareness of what really is. Most of the time we are not aware. We can walk beside a rugged mountain range, along a trail, beside a brook, and the whole time we are thinking of the latest mystery novel we are reading. We are in conversation with a friend, but our concentration is on the bills we have to pay and our fear that we will not be able to do so. Our decision as Christians is to become aware in ordinary life and in the spiritual life. Thelma Hall identifies some of the obstacles that hinder us from being aware of God, of the world around us, and of other people.

- *Preconceptions*: We see what we expect to see. If we don't anticipate that we will connect on a deep level with a particular person, chances are we do not connect. If we do not expect to meet God in any way except through our thoughts, chances are we will not be aware of God's presence in the center of our being.

- *Preoccupation*: We live in the past (with our regrets) or in the future (with our anticipations), but we let the present slip by unnoticed. We get distracted by lesser concerns. We live fragmented lives. No wonder we find it difficult to focus on others or on God in a way that allows us to connect.[2]

We cannot manufacture contemplation, but we can be silent and aware. We practice it by remaining silent before God—not thinking, not thinking about not thinking, just resting. Silence is difficult for us to achieve in our overstimulated world. It is enough simply to stay in the silence.

Daily Lectio

In the week ahead, read through Luke 14:12-24. This is the parable of the great banquet with its call to involvement in the world of people.

Luke 14 contains a collection of stories about banquets, which Jesus uses to teach various lessons. In the first story (verses 12-14), Jesus teaches about generosity. He encourages the invitation of the misfits of society to your banquet. They will be unable to return the favor. In this way, your reward is in heaven, not in receiving an invitation in return to a banquet staged by one of your guests.

This bit of advice sparks a comment from one of the guests who points out that there will be a great banquet in the kingdom of God. In response, Jesus tells a parable in which a question is raised: would you actually attend such a banquet or would you allow other concerns to sidetrack you? In this parable (verses 15-24), the host has issued invitations that have, apparently, been accepted. But when he finishes preparations and sends his servants around to tell the guests that everything is ready, they make excuses for not coming.

Jesus identifies three excuses. In the first instance, a man pleads that he must go off to see the field he has just bought—as if anyone would buy a field sight unseen. The second man says he has to try out his new oxen—as if this test of their abilities could not wait. The third pleads that he must remain at home because he just got married. This is a reference to Old Testament law that allows a man to avoid military service for the first year of his marriage. It says nothing about avoiding social contact. In response, the host scours the poorer sections of the city and invites the downtrodden. When not enough are found there, he widens the radius of the search to the countryside, giving his servants instructions to "compel" them to come. They will need convincing that they are actually being invited to a grand banquet.

In this way Jesus defines the mission of the church: to invite people to God's great banquet, both those inside the city and those outside the city. As such, this parable speaks to our own part in issuing such an invitation. It is not by accident that our work is to be among the needy and outcast. To follow Jesus is to engage in his work. It is to move beyond a life of safety and comfort with the message of Jesus. Another point of this parable is that we must not resist this gracious invitation by getting sidetracked with lesser concerns.

Work through this passage using the *lectio divina* method of study and prayer.

Notes

1. Thelma Hall, *Too Deep for Words: Rediscovering Lectio Divina* (New York: Paulist Press, 1988), p. 2.
2. Hall, p. 115.

Outcomes of *Lectio Divina*

What is the value of *lectio divina?* For one thing, we need to distinguish between short-term gain and long-term gain. In the short term we gain a new way of Bible study and prayer—a method that serves us well in our attempt to hear God through Scripture. Also we will have a new experience of the presence of God. We will receive guidance from God through Scripture. This can only be an encouragement to us.

In the long term we hope to gain transformation. This discipline has a cumulative effect. Over time we become different people—more open to God, certainly, but also more open to others and their needs and more aware of the world around us.

We should see differences in our relationships. When we experience God's love for us (as we do in the process of contemplative Bible reading), we are able to love others more freely. Being loved allows us to love. We should find that we can let go of some of our old hatreds and angers. This is the beginning of healing. We become more aware. In learning to be aware of God, we learn to be aware of others. We become more sensitive to others, and this affects how we react. Through *lectio divina* we will not become perfect, but we should become better.

Perhaps the biggest outcome is that Scripture comes alive for us in new ways. Whereas we once read the text to understand it with our minds, now we encounter Scripture on a new level. Now we open ourselves to be changed by what we have come to understand. Our encounter with Scripture becomes an encounter with God through prayer. We pray what we read. Prayer becomes easier and more natural in that it flows directly out of our reflection.

What benefits us most is not the rigid application of each *lectio* step, but the acceptance of the process into our lives.

- ❖ We learn to approach a passage in Scripture prayerfully, asking God to speak to us through it. We have new expectation when we come to the Bible. We know the power of reading the passage aloud and have learned to listen carefully.

- ❖ We learn to mull over what we hear in such a way that we identify how it connects with our lives. Meditation becomes a reflex.

- ❖ We learn to offer what we discover to God in prayer. Bible reading and prayer become one process.

- ❖ We learn to stay open to God in the silence of prayer. We learn about deep resting in the presence of God but do not feel guilty if that does not happen. We know prayer is what God gives us.

So far we have considered the impact of *lectio divina* on us personally. But this discipline has an impact on those around us as well, as Theodor Bovet explains:

> Each teacher, each worker, each statesman, who does not listen to God, but rather is bound to a divisive system, denotes great danger for many. On the other hand, every housewife, every laborer, or every doctor who listens to God, disseminates love, joy, and peace round about himself, and God's triumph in the world is accomplished through him.[1]

In the end, the old monks are right. We seek God in this way because it is our calling to seek God. We do not necessarily become happier or richer or even more fulfilled because we practice *lectio divina*. But then, these have never been the measures of success in God's kingdom. We will, however, know God better and experience God's love as a reality in our lives and not just as a concept we espouse.

Note

1. Theodor Bovet, *Have Time and Be Free* (London: S.P.C.K., 1965), p. 56.

A Select Bibliography

Aigner, Jill, O.S.B. *Foundations Last Forever: Lectio Divina, A Mode of Scripture Prayer*. Mt. Angel, OR: Priory Production, 1987.

Bovet, Theodor. *Have Time and Be Free: Toward the Organization of One's Life*. trans. by A. J. Ungersma. London: S.P.C.K., 1965.

Cousins, Kathryn and Ewert, with Richard J. Payne. *How to Read a Spiritual Book*. New York: Paulist Press, 1981.

Hall, Thelma. *Too Deep for Words: Rediscovering Lectio Divina*. New York: Paulist Press, 1988.

Leclercq, Jean. *The Love of Learning and the Desire for God: A Study of Monastic Culture*. New York: Fordham University Press, 1982 (especially chapters 1 and 5).

Mulholland, M. Robert, Jr. *Shaped by the Word: The Power of Scripture in Spiritual Formation*. Nashville, TN: The Upper Room, 1985.

Muto, Susan Annette. *A Practical Guide to Spiritual Reading*. rev. ed. Petersham, MA: St. Bede's Publications, 1994.

O'Donnell, Gabriel, O.P. "Reading for Holiness: Lectio Divina" in *Spiritual Traditions for the Contemporary Church*. eds. Gabriel O'Donnell and Robin Maas. Nashville, TN: Abingdon, 1990, pages 45-54.

Shannon, William H. *Seeking the Face of God*. New York: Crossroad, 1990.

Smith, Michael J. *The Word Is Very Near You: A Guide to Praying the Scripture*. Cambridge, MA: Cowley Publications, 1989.

Vest, Norvene. *Bible Reading for Spiritual Growth*. San Francisco: HarperSanFrancisco, 1993.

LEADER'S NOTES FOR THIS STUDY

If you are the small group leader, it is important for you to read "The Art of Leadership" below. In addition, before each session, go over the notes for that session.

The Art of Leadership

It's not difficult to be a small group leader. All you need is

- ❖ the willingness to lead,
- ❖ the commitment to read through all of the materials prior to the session,
- ❖ the sensitivity to others that will allow you to guide the discussion without dominating it, and
- ❖ the willingness to be used by God as a small group leader.

It's also not hard to start a small group. All it takes is the willingness of one person to make some phone calls. When you invite people to join the group, be sure to explain how the group will operate since this is a different kind of small group. See "How to Use This Guide" on pages 7-10 and "The Spiritual Formation Series" on pages 111-112, which together explain the nature of this group.

It is more important to meet in the right sort of place for this group than for most small groups. The key issue is silence. You cannot do group *lectio divina* except in a quiet place. You will need a home or room where children, pets, and the telephone will not interrupt your sessions.

Here are some basic small group principles that will help you do your job.

Ask the questions: Let group members respond.

Guide the discussion: Ask follow-up questions (or make comments) that draw others into the discussion and keep the discussion going. For example: "John, how would you answer the question?" or "Anybody else have any insights into this question?"

Start and stop on time: If you don't, people may be hesitant to come again because they never know when they will get home.

Stick to the time allotted to each section: There is always more that can be said in response to any question. It's your job to make sure the discussion keeps moving from question to question. Remember: it's better to cut off discussion when it's going well than to let it go on until it dies out. There are two times given for each section of the group meeting. The first time is for groups that last sixty minutes; the second is for ninety-minute groups.

Model answers to questions: Whenever you ask a question to which everyone is expected to respond (for example, an open question as opposed to a Bible study question), you, as leader, should be the first person to respond. In this way you model the right length—and appropriate level—of response.

Understand the intention of different kinds of questions:

- ❖ *Experience questions*: The aim is to cause people to recall past experiences and share these memories with the group. There are no right or wrong answers to these questions. They facilitate the group process by getting people to share their stories and to think about the topic.

- ❖ *Forced-choice questions*: Certain questions will be followed by a series of suggested answers (with check-boxes). Generally, there is no "correct" answer. Options aid group members and guide their responses.

- *Questions with multiple parts*: Sometimes a question is asked and then various aspects of it are listed below. Ask the group members to answer each of the sub-questions. Their answers, taken together, will answer the initial question.

- *Analysis questions*: These force the group to notice what the Bible text says and to explore it for meaning.

- *Application questions*: These help the group make connections between the meaning of the text and their own lives.

Introduce each section: This may involve a brief overview of the focus, purpose, and topic of the new section and instructions on how to do the exercise.

Guide the exercises: A major portion of your job will be guiding the Bible study or the group *lectio*. Try to familiarize yourself with the group *lectio* process before you have to lead it the first time. Details of how to lead each section will be found below, especially in the material on the first meeting.

Comment: Occasionally bring into the discussion some useful information from your own study. Keep your comments brief. Don't allow yourself to become the "expert" to whom everyone turns for "the right answer."

Session One: Longing for God/ Bible Study

Get enough copies of this book so that each person has one. The book contains all the information needed for each of the small group sessions as well as information on the process of contemplative Bible reading.The first session is crucial. People will be deciding whether they want to be a part of the group. So your aim as leader is to

- generate vision about this particular group (so that each person will want to continue in the group),

- give people an overview of the whole series (so they will know where the group is headed),

- build relationships (so that a sense of community starts to develop), and

- encourage commitment to being a part of the group (so that everyone will return next week, bringing along a friend!).

Potluck

A good way to launch the first session of any small group is by eating together prior to the session. Sharing a meal draws people together and breaks down barriers between them.

Ask everyone to bring along one dish for the supper. This makes it easy to have a meal for twelve. If you feel ambitious, though, you might want to invite everyone to dinner at your home. What you serve need not be elaborate. Conversation, not dining, is the intention of the get-together.

The aim of the meal is to get to know one another in an informal setting. Structure the meal in such a way that a lot of conversation takes place.

After the meal, be sure to do the first session in a complete and full form (and not just talk about what you are going to do when the group starts). Your aim is to give everyone the experience of what it means to be a part of this small group.

Introduction to the First Session:

Welcome: Greet the group and let them know how glad you are that they have come and how much you look forward to being with them for the coming weeks.

Prayer: Pray briefly, thanking God for assembling this group. Ask God to guide your deliberations and sharing today and during the coming weeks. Pray that God will guide all of you in discovering the power of contemplative Bible reading to grow in your spiritual lives.

Group process: Describe how the small group will function and what it will study. Discuss, specifically:

❖ *Series theme*: The aim is to learn how to do contemplative Bible reading, both in a group and individually.

❖ *Group experience*: Describe how you will alternate between a Bible study one week and an experience of group *lectio* the next week. Talk about the opening exercises (to assist the group in knowing one another), discussion, and prayer together as you hear God's Word.

❖ *Group details*: Describe where you will meet, when, and how long each session will last.

❖ *Group aims*: The hope is that each person's spiritual growth will be enhanced by learning this new spiritual discipline.

Do session one using the material in the book and following the instructions in the next section.

Overview: The role of each overview section is to provide a road map for the group through the material. Small groups work better when everyone is informed about where the group is going and what steps will be taken to get there. Begin each new small group session with a quick look at the overview so that the group will have a sense of the whole before the study starts.

Open: The aim of this exercise is twofold: to begin the process of getting to know one another and to think about how we have done Bible study in the past. The first question asks the group to tell a little of their stories to one another. Such sharing is the key to developing community. The second and third questions start the group thinking about the topic of Bible study as they begin the process of learning (what will be for some) a new way of Bible study: contemplative Bible reading.

Watch the time carefully. It is easy to spend more than the allotted twenty to thirty minutes because it is such fun sharing stories. Be sure to end on time. Otherwise you will not get through the Bible study. The important thing is *not* getting through all the questions in this module. The important thing is inviting each person to speak and to think about Bible study. Stop on time even if you have not covered all the questions.

The passage: You can either read this aloud or ask group members to read the passage silently.

Analysis: You could easily take an hour or more to discuss all this material. If you did this, the study would be thrown out of balance and you would never get to the heart of the experience: using the passage as a means of prayer. Your job as leader is to keep the study moving and to stay within the time limit for this part. You may have to skip some of the questions (which people could then use on their own during the week for personal study of the passage). But be sure to cover at least questions 4 and 5. Question 4 gives a good overview of the passage, and question 5 focuses on the portion of the psalm that will be used in the group *lectio divina* exercise.

Resonance: The aim in this session is to make connections between the lives of each person and the text. Question 9 is an overview question that asks the group to think about the application of this psalm. The other questions connect with the themes.

Prayer: The conclusion to Bible study is prayer.

Bible study notes: These can be used by the group during the session or read individually afterward. As group leader you need to go over these several times. They will help you guide the discussion. (Many of the notes end with questions in case you'd like the group to continue reflecting on the passage.)

Conclusion: Draw attention to the material in the rest of the session. Suggest that people read carefully the Bible study notes as they think about Psalm 63. Invite them to read the essay on their own (and pages 11-20 if they have not already done so). In each *lectio* session, the essay addresses one of the steps of contemplative Bible reading. These essays expand group members' understanding of each aspect of the process. You may decide to read and discuss these essays together as a group.

In particular, invite people to do daily *lectio* during the week as they are able. Beginning in session four, the opening exercise will involve sharing what one finds in daily *lectio*.

Session Two: Longing for God/*Lectio* Exercise

Group lectio: During the first experience of group *lectio* it will be very important that you as leader have looked over the instructions carefully. Make sure you know what to do at each point because it will be up to you to guide the process. In fact, you might wish to practice leading the group, imagining each step and saying aloud the words you will use to move from step to step. Make sure you have a watch to time the periods of silence. It is hard to correctly gauge the proper length for silence without a watch. Stick to the times given.

It also will be important for you to find two volunteers beforehand to do the second and third readings. You will do the first reading (in which you will read the passage twice). Instruct the two volunteers to read the passage slowly and thoughtfully, making no other comments. Guide the group with deliberation. The group needs to know that someone understands the entire process and will guide them, so they do not have to fear what comes next. Honor the right to pass.

At first, it may be necessary to interrupt group members who get off track or take too long. You might "warn" the group that you will be "keeping the process on schedule" and that this might involve interruptions. Do this with a sense of humor and kindness. It is important that the process be followed quite closely, especially when the group is learning it.

Discussion: How long you have for this session will depend on how many people you have in the group. Do this first experience of group *lectio* all together, using as much time as you need (and using what time is left, if any, for discussion). In subsequent weeks you may want to split into two sub-groups if you have more than ten people in your group. Come back together as a single group for this discussion.

Use the questions to guide a general discussion. That is, unlike the open exercise which is a circle response with everyone participating, throw this open to general discussion.

Remember that because this is a new exercise for most group members, there will be questions about process ("I wasn't sure what to do when we came to the invitation part"). Do not feel you need to have expert answers to such questions. Let group members share their experiences.

Essay: This is to be read as part of the homework. Discuss it along with the daily *lectio* exercise at the end of the session.

Daily lectio: Encourage people to try this process on their own. The passages chosen complement the passage studied in the small group session.

Note:
The notes that follow for the remainder of the sessions will be briefer than the notes for session one, because the process is the same for each group session. Only those sections that involve new things will be commented upon. If you have questions about how to lead any session, consult notes from session one or two.

Session Three: The Call of Jesus/Bible Study

Open: This will be a different sort of discussion. It looks at the question of a small group covenant and not at the experience of group members. It is an important session because a group covenant binds the group together.

The passage: You shift from analyzing a psalm to analyzing a story. The type of questions you use are a little different. Watch the time carefully in the analysis section. You may not get to all the questions. Use enough questions so that the group has a good feel for what this passage is about. If you go overtime in the analysis section, you will not have enough time for the important issues in the resonance section.

Conclusion: Remind people to work on daily *lectio*. They will be invited to share their reflections during the "Open" exercise in the next group session.

Session Four: The Call of Jesus/*Lectio* Exercise

Open: A new type of opening exercise is introduced today. Rather than following an exercise designed to introduce the topic through past experiences, you are asking the group to "check in." In this exercise, group members share experiences or encounters with the text because the last session. While this does not introduce the topic of the session, the sharing has the advantage of being fresh and real. When group members know that they will be asked to share about how well they are doing in their daily *lectio*, they are more apt to do daily *lectio*! The aim of this open exercise is not to shame anyone into doing daily *lectio*. It offers to the group the results of others' *lectio* reflections. Make sure group members know that it is permissible to say, "Pass," when it comes their turn to share.

Group lectio: Notice that there are new instructions about the process of group *lectio*. At this point in most group *lectio* sessions you will find a brief comment on one aspect of the process. This is the way I have chosen to add information about group *lectio*. Once again, it is important for you to give strong and confident leadership to the process. It is up to you to guide each step. It is particularly important when the group is learning this process that you give them the comfort of knowing that someone understands it and is guiding them carefully.

Discussion: This is an important part of the process. Having done group *lectio* together, now you step back and discuss the experience. Let the group learn from one another how to do *lectio*. Also let the group share with one another its impact on their lives. This is how community grows. The more you share and the longer you are together in this way, the deeper the bonds become. This is important because we were never meant to grow spiritually on our own. We need each other. A caring community is the ideal environment in which to grow.

Today you have two tasks:

- Continue the discussion of process. It is still early in the learning curve.

Some people may be unclear about aspects of the process. Invite questions and observations. In particular, ask people about their experience of daily *lectio*. Is it working? Is it making sense? Again, use wisdom as you wrestle with questions and observations. Help the group to meld their experiences together.

❖ Begin the process of group discernment. As explained in the instructions heading this section, this is a way of testing out what we think we are hearing from God. Not only does this have value as a way of discernment (is this really from God?), but it is also a way to encourage and motivate. As group members share what they are working on, group accountability develops.

Session Five: The Cost of Discipleship/Bible Study

Open: You have only two questions instead of the usual three, but this will be enough to get a lively discussion going. This is a "what-if" exercise that helps us examine values.

Session Six: The Cost of Discipleship/*Lectio* Exercise

You might want to inquire how the group is doing in reading the essays. These are an important part of learning about *lectio divina*.

Session Seven: The Priorities of Life/Bible Study

Open: This is a different sort of exercise, which should be both fun and useful for your group. It has two parts. Part one is the determination of type. Give everyone a few minutes to read over the categories and make choices. Each person must choose (and not sit on the fence) in each of the four categories. Tell the person who says, "both categories fit me" or "some in one category and others in the other category fit me" that he or she must pick the category that is marginally more descriptive of who they are. Don't let people worry about "doing it right" (this is a fun exercise, not a serious analysis). At the end of the first question, everybody needs a set of four letters (in the order in which the questions are asked) like ENTJ or ISFP. (There are actually sixteen possible combinations of letters.)

You don't have to be a Myers-Briggs Type Indicator (MBTI) expert to do this exercise. In fact, you do not need to know anything about the test. However, there is probably someone in your small group who understands the MBTI and can help with this exercise. If anyone expresses an interest in taking the evaluation, you should encourage them to do so.

The aim of the second and third questions is to get discussion going that will display that we do have different temperaments. There are not good or bad temperaments, only different temperaments. And these temperaments mean we look at issues differently. Do not worry about answering these questions fully. The point is to get group members talking about the different ways each views an issue. Make this fun.

Watch your time carefully. This kind of exercise can gobble up a lot of time if you do not rein in discussion. Remember the function of the opening exercise, and keep the discussion in line with its function.

Analysis: Your first task is to read the text carefully enough to glean all the information about the type of people Mary and Martha are. Then get the group to discuss from that data. They have met people like each of these women, so they can fill in the missing details.

Resonance: The issue you want to focus on is how the approach to life differs among group members and in what different ways the text is challenging them. There is no such thing as the ideal approach. In the midst of our different approaches we need to discern "the one thing needed."

Session Nine: The Courage of Faith/Bible Study

Analysis: Rather than ferreting out the facts and finding the meaning (as you have been doing in the Analysis sections), you are asked to "imagine what it was like." Actually, this is just another way of noticing what is in the text and then piecing it all together into a whole that makes sense. The outcome is the same; the process is different. Your aim as the small group leader is to guide the discussion so that as a group you paint a picture of this most provocative setting. The result is that you understand this text in a deeper way than ever before. It is one thing to know in your mind that Peter walked on water; it is another to feel his fear and his exhilaration as he stepped out of the boat, to feel the spray in his face, the wind pushing against him as he strode toward Jesus.

Resonance: These three questions are more open-ended than what you have used in the past: no options to choose from, no suggested answers. This is intentional. By this time the group should be well established. A level of trust exists. Most importantly, this is a group that has been listening to God. These are the kinds of questions that cause us to identify, reflect upon, and share the hints and intimations drawn from our time with God. To follow Jesus is to be challenged to go in directions we might not have thought of on our own.

Session Ten: The Courage of Faith/*Lectio* Exercise

This session includes some exercises to bring the group to closure.

The Spiritual Formation Series

Four themes weave their way through the Spiritual Formation study guides by Richard Peace: story, pilgrimage, community, and disciplines.

Story

We all have a story. Our stories give us identity. They tell who we are because they chart the unfolding of our lives and the factors that make each of us unique.

But we do not always know our stories. There are various reasons why our stories may be murky or incomprehensible.

❖ *Inattention*: We let life pass us by. Each day comes and goes, and we hardly notice. Because our minds are not focused on what is happening in and to us, our days go unrecorded.

❖ *Pain*: Our lives are too painful to notice. Not noticing is our way of coping. If we noticed we would cry out in agony.

❖ *No grid*: We do not notice the texture of our lives because we have no categories for talking about our lives. Life just happens.

❖ *No friends*: We do not know our stories because we have never talked about them with anyone else. Perhaps we are shy, or we may be part of a group that does not talk about such things. Or we may tell only certain kinds of personal stories (about kids or job) but leave most of our lives undiscussed.

Not knowing our stories, we do not understand them. Our lives are a mystery to us. We do not understand our anger or our needs or even our desires. We cannot anticipate our responses or plan our futures. We are left with only the immediate—the here and now—and that, too, soon passes from our consciousness. Nor do we have any way of making sense of our stories. We do not know they have any significance beyond ourselves. We do not connect our stories with God's story.

Of course, some people have a clear sense of their stories. But even they can be enriched when they hear others' stories. In relationship, they discover new meaning. In the telling of their stories, they are affirmed in who they are.

Pilgrimage

Our stories are not random. In fact, to be a follower of Jesus is to walk in his way. This way is not some vague path. It is a well-marked road first walked by Jesus, the author and pioneer of our faith, then walked by the Twelve and others in the first century, and later walked by countless men and women through time—people from different ages and cultures. Our ancestors have left us ample records about the way. We are pilgrims on a journey. Our story becomes the story of our pilgrimage.

When we understand that we are part of a glorious company called the people of God, we have a new frame of reference. Now the question becomes, Are we living in the way that brings wholeness to us and others? Is this God's wholeness?

Community

Through our stories we come into community with others. I believe that the basis of community is found in sharing our stories with one another. It is difficult to disdain someone whose story you have heard. As we listen to each other's stories, we see the links and we connect, especially when we share a commitment to a common story.

The uniqueness of our community lies in the fact that we actively connect our stories with God's story. We evaluate our stories on the basis of what we read in the Bible. We actively relate to others who are walking in Jesus' way.

The pilgrimage of God's people was never meant to be solitary. We walk our pilgrimage in the company of others who help us and receive our help. We are family, so it is not surprising that we would learn spiritual disciplines in the company of others.

Disciplines

The spiritual disciplines are simply ways of living that enable us to become like Christ. By practicing these disciplines, we train ourselves to respond to life as Jesus would. In particular, the spiritual disciplines keep us alert to the presence of God.

We can easily lose our awareness of God's immediacy in the familiarity of routine. Worship, Bible reading, time with others, and even prayer become ends in themselves, not paths to the presence of God. God's voice is muted. Or it gets covered by unexamined cultural or personal baggage. The spiritual disciplines are ways of sorting out the voices that would distract us from noticing the Voice. They also enable us to communicate with God and to grow spiritually.